THE HOLOCAUST ACROSS GENERATIONS

The Holocaust across Generations

Trauma and Its Inheritance among Descendants of Survivors

Janet Jacobs

NEW YORK UNIVERSITY PRESS
New York

NEW YORK UNIVERSITY PRESS
New York
www.nyupress.org

© 2016 by New York University
All rights reserved

References to Internet websites (URLs) were accurate at the time of writing. Neither the author nor New York University Press is responsible for URLs that may have expired or changed since the manuscript was prepared.

Library of Congress Cataloging-in-Publication Data
Names: Jacobs, Janet Liebman, author.
Title: The Holocaust across generations : trauma and its inheritance among descendants of survivors / Janet Jacobs.
Description: New York ; London : New York University Press, [2016] | Includes bibliographical references and index.
Identifiers: LCCN 2016023896 | ISBN 978-1-4798-3356-6 (cl : alk. paper) | ISBN 978-1-4798-3929-2 (pb : alk. paper)
Subjects: LCSH: Holocaust, Jewish (1939-1945)—Psychological aspects. | Holocaust survivors—Psychology. | Children of Holocaust survivors—Mental health. | Holocaust, Jewish (1939-1945)—Social aspects. | Intergenerational communication—Case studies.
Classification: LCC RC451.4.H62 J33 2016 | DDC 616.85/210089924—dc23
LC record available at https://lccn.loc.gov/2016023896

New York University Press books are printed on acid-free paper, and their binding materials are chosen for strength and durability. We strive to use environmentally responsible suppliers and materials to the greatest extent possible in publishing our books.

Manufactured in the United States of America

10 9 8 7 6 5 4 3 2 1

Also available as an ebook

For survivors, for those who come after, and for SBL

CONTENTS

Acknowledgments   ix

Introduction   1

1. Family Narratives and the Social Construction of Descendant Identity   13
2. Ritual and the Emotional Transmission of Holocaust Trauma   41
3. Redefining the Sacred: Spirituality and the Crisis of Masculinity among Children and Grandchildren of Survivors   65
4. The Social Relations of Inherited Trauma: The Meaning of Attachment and Connection in the Lives of Descendants   83
5. Reengaging the Past: Identity, Mourning, and Empathy at Sites of Terror   105
6. Descendants as Holocaust Carriers: Bringing the Past into Public Consciousness   125

Conclusion: The Changing Landscape of Holocaust Remembrance and Future Directions in the Study of Traumatic Inheritance   149

Notes   159

Bibliography   161

Index   173

About the Author   179

ACKNOWLEDGMENTS

I am deeply grateful to the descendants of Holocaust survivors who so openly and generously shared their life stories with me. From the outset, this project asked a great deal of the participants—children and grandchildren of survivors who in the course of the research relived the pain of their families' past while revealing their own complicated and multilayered experiences within survivor culture. Throughout the project, the insights and thoughtfulness that the descendants brought to the research setting provided an invaluable intellectual and emotional resource for my own developing interpretations and understanding of traumatic transference. Without their willingness to explore the intergenerational transmission of trauma, this book would not have been possible.

I also thank all those who offered encouragement at various and crucial points along the way. Among those to whom I am especially grateful are Shawn Landres, Mary Jo Neitz, Paul Shankman, and Rhys Williams. I am also grateful to Charles Hyman, Betty Jane Jacobs, Linda Loewenstein, and Jonathan Oldham for their help and particular contributions to the project. I remember with deep gratitude Donald Capps, whose mentorship, generosity, and kindness remain a source of inspiration.

I thank Stephanie Bonnes, Leith Lombas, and Zachary Owens for their research assistance. I am deeply appreciative of the wise counsel and patience of my editor, Jennifer Hammer, whose advice and guidance were indispensable to the completion of the book.

Last, I am indebted to my family for their unfailing support. Thank you especially to my partner, Gary, and to Jamie, Michael, Spencer, and Eric. I am profoundly grateful for Felix, Brecken, Ryan, and River, who remind me always that the past does not have to repeat itself.

Introduction

The study of the Holocaust has taken many turns and directions over the past two decades, generating a plethora of scholarship across a wide range of orientations from historical analysis to the social-psychological effects of mass trauma on individuals, groups, and society. Within this extensive and far-reaching field of research, the intergenerational transmission of trauma has become a particularly significant area of study that continues to inform the way in which scholars address and understand the reproduction of trauma-based knowledge and emotions across generations. Since the 1960s and 1970s, the children of Holocaust survivors have been recognized as members of a unique population who have "inherited" the psychic markers of those who lived through and survived a horrific past. Early on in the study of the intergenerational transmission of trauma, the psychological studies in the field confirmed that the suffering and wounds of genocide do not end or disappear when the threat of death and annihilation no longer exists. Rather, the research found that the traumas of the past remain embedded in the psychic life of victims whose emotions, memories, behaviors, and thoughts are passed on to descendant generations. According to the plentiful and diverse scholarship in the field, this process of traumatic transference has resulted in the creation of successive generations of trauma carriers whose lives and social actions remain deeply connected to the genocidal history of the Nazi regime (Bar-On 1995; Herman 1997; Baranowsky et al. 1998; Binder-Byrnes et al. 1998).

In a departure from the heavily psychological orientation of previous research, the primary interest of this book is on the social structures through which the trauma of the Holocaust is conveyed to the children and grandchildren of survivors who today constitute the first and second generation of Holocaust descendants. Through an exploration into family narratives, belief structures, and social relations, this work reveals the multiple social forces that shape and inform the worldviews of descendants and the diverse ways in which descendancy is understood and expressed by succeeding generations. Using the social frameworks that highlight the study of relationality, social interaction, and the transmission of family memory and history, this book offers new perspectives on the social meanings of the Holocaust and the formation of "communities of memory" (Kidron 2003, 515) among both first- and second-generation descendants who retain the knowledge and feeling states of a terrible past.

Expanding on the extensive psychological literature and the foundational sociological scholarship (Gottschalk 2003; Stein 2009a), this volume contributes to the field of genocide and Holocaust studies in a number of important ways: (1) through an exploration into the social structures by which the experiences and memory of trauma are transmitted across generations; (2) through an examination of the social relations of traumatic inheritance among survivors and their adult children and grandchildren; and (3) through an investigation into the formation of trauma-based identities among Holocaust carrier groups. Significantly, the book comes at a crucial time in the study of genocide and the transmission of Holocaust trauma. As the number of survivors has vastly diminished over time, their children and now their grandchildren are seeking ways to better understand and connect to their families' traumatic past. This work sheds light on this growing trend among Holocaust descendants and the social impact of descendancy on the preservation of Holocaust memory for the wider society.

Descendants as Research Participants: Methods and Respondent Backgrounds

The research for this book began more than a decade ago, when I undertook a qualitative study of children of Holocaust survivors. Initially, my contacts with descendant populations began with two Children of Holocaust Survivors organizations that met regularly to share their experiences and to create friendships and social support systems with others who had grown up in a post-Holocaust family environment. In approaching the organizations, I explained that I was interested in studying the intergenerational transmission of trauma and, if permissible, would like to attend their meetings and interview members of the organizations. Both groups were open to my research and invited me to their events and social gatherings. Additionally, the majority of group members agreed to be interviewed individually. From these initial contacts with first-generation descendants, snowball sampling led to an expansion of the research population and to the inclusion of grandchildren of survivors who, as an emerging generation of Holocaust culture bearers, currently represent a new and important descendant carrier group.

Altogether, I interviewed seventy-five descendants: sixty children of survivors (thirty-three women and twenty-seven men) between the ages of forty-six and sixty-two and fifteen grandchildren (nine men and six women) between the ages of twenty and thirty-two. Among these, two of the respondents crossed categories. In one case, the respondent was both a child and grandchild of survivors and in another the respondent was both a survivor and a child of survivors. The vast majority of interviews took place in one of four regions in the United States, including the East and West coasts, the Midwest, and the Rocky Mountains. Although most of the participants had been raised in the United States, four of the participants were born in Europe and emigrated to the United States during adolescence or young adulthood. Six others were born in displaced-persons camps in Germany and came to the United States as young children. Three participants are citizens of other countries. Of these, one respondent lives in the Balkan region of eastern Europe, where the interview took place, and the other two are Israeli and were living in the United States at the time of the interview. In close to three-quarters of the cases, both parents or grandparents were Holocaust survivors, a demographic that is consistent with a postwar trend in which survivors tended to marry one another. In two cases, however, the survivor married into a family with ties to Nazi Germany and thus the extended family of the participant included war-time Nazi sympathizers, although the marriage took place after the war had ended.

While all of the participants identified as descendants of survivors, the nature of survivorship varied across families. For the purposes of the research, the concept of survivorship included a broad range of experiences that reflect the descendants' varied understanding of what it means for a parent and/or grandparent to have lived through or in some way been directly and personally affected by the Holocaust. In a small number of cases, family members survived through immigration, escape, hiding, and passing as non-Jews. In a larger number of cases, family members had been incarcerated in labor and/or death camps. The differences in the backgrounds of the survivor families were further evident in their varied nationalities. In this respect, the parents and grandparents of the respondents included Jews from Poland, Russia, Germany, Lithuania, the Czech Republic, Slovakia, Croatia, France, and Italy, an expanse of Europe and eastern European countries that is a stark reminder of the extent to which Nazi domination threatened the survival of European Jewry. Further, the sample population included one non-Jewish first-generation descendant who strongly identified as a child of Holocaust survivors. This participant, who was born in a displaced-persons camp in Germany, was the daughter of eastern European parents who had been deported to a Nazi slave labor camp, where they remained until liberation. When I first came into contact with this participant, she explained that she had previously attended Children of Survivors meetings. I chose to include her in the study to illuminate the diverse cultural links that exist within the history of Holocaust trauma and its transmission across generations, religions, and nationalities.

In addition to these background differences, the religious upbringing of the Jewish participants was also varied and diverse. Nearly half of the respondents were raised in Conservative Jewish homes. Among the other half, eighteen of the respondents were raised as Orthodox Jews;

sixteen as Reform Jews; six without any denominational affiliation; three as atheists; and two as non-Jews. At the time of the interview, eight of the respondents identified as Orthodox Jews; eighteen as Conservative Jews; fourteen as Reform Jews; six as followers of Jewish Renewal (a modern-day egalitarian movement that has its roots in Hasidism); and twelve as Jewish spiritual seekers who had not yet found a synagogue or movement with which to affiliate. Eight described themselves as unaffiliated Jews and four claimed no religious identification. One Jewish respondent identified as Catholic, two as Unitarian, and two as Buddhist. Regardless of current religious affiliation, however, all of the Jewish respondents identified as ethnic if not religious Jews.

In conducting the interviews, I used a life history approach. Following a semi-structured interview format, the interview schedule included open-ended questions about family history, knowledge of the Holocaust, religious upbringing, and current spiritual beliefs and practices. Participants were also asked how they first learned of their families' survivor backgrounds and who in their family passed on the knowledge and memories of the Holocaust to them. Other questions focused on their perceptions of themselves as descendants of Holocaust survivors and their connection to the traumas of their parents and grandparents. The interviews were conducted under conditions of confidentiality and generally lasted between two and four hours. All the interviews were recorded and then transcribed for analysis.

The majority of the interviews took place in the homes of the participants. Because of the familial location of the interview sites, the respondents frequently shared photographs, family documents, and family artifacts that had survived the war. In some instances the process of sharing led to tours through a participant's home, as he or she pointed out framed photographs of parents or grandparents before and after the war and of other family members who did not survive. At other times, respondents produced surviving Nazi documents, such as identity cards, or carefully assembled scrapbooks that chronicled the family's ordeal and survival. Thus, the settings of the interviews were, in many cases, field sites in and of themselves—spaces of memory and family culture where recollections of the past and narratives of childhood were enhanced by familial surroundings that enriched and recalled the respondents' ties to loss, survival, and catastrophe. In two instances, descendants shared videos they had made while visiting sites of terror with family members in Europe. During these viewings, the descendants narrated the videos, recalling the feelings they experienced during these tours and the physical spaces that these sites memorialized.

Because more than half of the first-generation descendants had some affiliation with Children of Survivors organizations, they constitute a self-selected group of participants who have been part of an ongoing social movement that recognizes the noteworthy role that children of survivors play as carriers of Holocaust trauma both for themselves and within the larger culture. The origins of this movement have been tied to the collective identity movements of the 1960s and 1970s, when the children of survivors began to examine their distinct experiences and perspectives as the descendants of Holocaust survivors (Berger 1997; Stein 2009b). Since then the Children of Survivors movement has grown into a widespread social network with national and local affiliates that serve as support groups for descendants of Holocaust survivors and as liaison organizations for Holocaust commemorative programs and ceremonies (Kidron 2003; DeGloma 2009). More recently, grandchildren of Holocaust survivors have also begun forming their own groups and currently have a Facebook page. A portion of those who affiliate with these multigeneration descendant movements self-identify as second- and third-generation survivors. Others, less comfortable with the term *survivor*, prefer to be called children or grandchildren of Holocaust survivors, or descendants of survivors. With the exception of quoted material where participants used the term *survivor* to describe themselves or others of their generation, the participants in this volume will be referred to as children, grandchildren, and/or first- and second-generation descendants of survivors.

In addition to the in-depth interviews, I also conducted participant observation at Holocaust commemorative events to observe and gather data on descendants as social actors. For the most part, these events took place in large and small synagogues in communities across the United States and in schools and universities in the western region of the country. Immediately following my attendance at these events, I recorded copious field notes on participant interaction, ceremonial acts, and my own impressions of Holocaust remembrance as it is observed and performed in the United States. During this period of data collection, I documented the structure of the commemorative events, the visual and narrative representations of the past that these events highlighted, and the role of survivors and descendants in shaping the memory of Holocaust trauma.

Other fieldwork sites included museums that exhibited descendant art and eastern European Jewish community centers. In addition, I studied descendants' memoirs and published writings. The diversity of data that I collected for this research (in-depth interviews, participant observation at Holocaust remembrance events, descendant writings, and artistic production) reflects the breadth and depth of the descendant phenomenon and the value of the social investigation into traumatic transference within a multigenerational framework.

Researching Traumatic Inheritance: Bonds of Ethnicity and Kinship

My interest in the intergenerational transmission of trauma evolved from my research on memorialization and collective memory. Having spent a number of years investigating the monuments and memorials to Nazi terror across the European landscape, I was keenly aware of how trauma becomes embedded in cultural narratives that reproduce for future generations the memory and events of genocidal suffering. Less clear to me was how the trauma of genocide, in all of its incomprehensibility, lives on within the culture of survivors who pass on these traumatic legacies to their children and grandchildren. Reaching back into my own childhood, I recognized that I was drawn to the study of traumatic transference in part because of my shared ethnicity with European Jews and in part because the Holocaust provided a backdrop to a Jewish upbringing that was quietly but persistently affected by the specter of loss and tragedy that the Holocaust evoked.

As a Jewish child born into the postwar culture of the United States, I found the Holocaust to be both overwhelmingly present and conspicuously absent in the Jewish community in which I was raised in the 1950s and 1960s. At Sunday school the Holocaust was the subtext for creating ties to the nascent State of Israel, and Sunday school was also the place where survivors, having only recently experienced the horrors of genocide, came to teach suburban children about their Jewish heritage. In this postwar Jewish community, survivors were also shopkeepers who ran delicatessens and bakeries that featured the kinds of food and delicacies that were reminiscent of their prewar lives and of a European Jewish culture that had been nearly destroyed. Thus, while the Holocaust was never far from the consciousness of this suburban community, the truth of the overwhelming tragedy was mostly left unspoken. These were the years before the advent of Holocaust commemoration, when a tattooed forearm, if acknowledged, was signified with silent gestures or whispers that alluded sorrowfully to "the camps," the word *camp* itself a code for a catastrophe that could not be named or described.

In my family, it was my maternal grandmother who indirectly and with little context referred to this silenced history. When I was not yet of school age, she would at times remove a tattered photograph from her apron pocket, pointing to two young girls with braided hair. Shaking her head, my grandmother would sigh heavily, speaking a combination of Yiddish and English phrases that I understood to mean "gone, all gone, the ovens, they're all gone." To this day, I do not know who these children were, though I have a vague impression that these young girls were sisters and their names may have been Anna and Rosa. I also remember my grandmother's looking at the photograph and then at me, as if I were somehow a reminder of their loss. But these recollections are not facts, only hazy memories of a little girl who felt her grandmother's despair and whose images of these forgotten children resurfaced as I delved more deeply into the study of Holocaust descendancy. As the research progressed, I recognized that I shared with the participants my own but much less defined and far removed traumatic inheritance, a kinship tie that remains at the heart of my personal connection to this work.

I completed this book in the same year as the seventieth anniversary of the liberation of Auschwitz. Nearly 300 survivors attended this major commemoration at Auschwitz, which was extensively covered by the international media. From thousands of miles away, I was able to observe a moving ceremony where aging survivors sat alongside their children and grandchildren as they listened to European dignitaries confront a regretful past and express hope for a better future. Having spent more than ten years interviewing the descendants of the survivors of Auschwitz and other Nazi camps, I was struck by the presence of the children and grandchildren who watched as their parents and grandparents recounted for the world, perhaps for the last time, a history of violation and dehumanization that reverberated throughout the memorial grounds of this iconic monument. In viewing the televised commemorations, I was brought back to the first interview I conducted for the study. The respondent was a woman in her fifties whose mother had survived Auschwitz as a 17-year-old girl. I remember clearly her first words, "My mother was a survivor of Auschwitz," and my unexpected response. For the first few moments of the interview, I felt as if I were sitting across not from the daughter of a survivor but from the survivor herself. The way in which the respondent told her mother's story, bringing the history and imagery of Auschwitz into sharp relief, created a slippage in time and place while I listened intently as she narrated her parent's traumatic past.

This initial experience was repeated time and again over my many years of research. Throughout the period of data collection, I was consistently struck by the depth with which the descendants spoke of the survivors' histories. Although not every participant could recount the exact details of a parent's or a grandparent's harrowing life during the Holocaust, a surprising number appeared to know when and how they were deported, what became of other family members, and how family members were able to survive under the most extreme and threatening circumstances. While, admittedly, there were gaps in these recollections, I was continually captivated by the emotional tone and historical knowledge that the descendants brought to the research setting. Typically, the respondent's engagement with the family history was all-consuming, revealing the power of memory, suffering, and self-awareness among descendants. Further, in reading and rereading the transcripts of their recorded narratives during the analytic phase of the project, my emotional engagement with the material grew in intensity as I gained a greater appreciation for the importance of trauma as an inherited legacy of an unwanted past.

The Scope of the Project and Thematic Content

Drawing on a diverse and multifaceted academic worldview, the overall content of the book focuses on the phenomenon of traumatic inheritance in a number of different areas of study that pertain to the social transmission of mass trauma and the legacy of the Holocaust among descendant populations. In bringing together an analysis of the social structures that affect the intergenerational transmission of trauma with research on the transference of emotions and identity between survivors and descendants, the work situates the scholarship on traumatic transference within a broadly construed sociological framework that draws on theories of identity formation, psycho-social development, interactional dynamics, memory, and trauma. As each of these areas of inquiry is developed and examined, the importance of gender to these social processes is considered along with a feminist perspective on the interdisciplinary nature of Holocaust studies. Within this wide-ranging and inclusive approach to the study of traumatic inheritance, a variety of themes and observations are presented throughout the book.

The first theme, which is elaborated in chapter 1, investigates the relationship between narrative and identity formation. Drawing on sociological theories of narrative and identity, this chapter analyzes the impact of survivor narratives on the construction of the descendant self and the tropes of victimization, heroism, and moral agency that characterize Holocaust storytelling. Chapter 2 then looks at the role of ritual as a vehicle for the exchange of emotion between survivors and descendants, highlighting the way in which feeling-states such as anger and sadness permeate ritual observance within survivor culture. Through an analysis of self-in-relation theory, this chapter examines emotional connectivity and the process of separation within the realm of ritual practice and innovation.

Following the discussion of ritual and emotion, chapter 3 considers the construction of spirituality and religious belief systems among descendants. In this chapter, the theme of alternative spirituality is explored and the principles of feminist theory are brought to bear on the descendants' disillusionment with biblical Judaism and the omnipotence of a patriarchal God. In chapter 4, the research turns to the social relations of attachment and connection among children and grandchildren of survivors. This chapter addresses familial tensions, extended family relationships, the realm of the supernatural, and the significance of place, as each of these dimensions of connectivity illuminate the types of attachments that give meaning to the socio-emotional lives of descendant populations.

Expanding on the importance of place in the consciousness of descendants, chapter 5 considers the role that sites of terror play in restructuring identity and attachment among descendants who engage with monuments and memorials to Nazi atrocities. Through an examination of immersion experiences at sites of terror, the findings illuminate how interactive spaces of memory shape identity, foster acts of mourning, and strengthen empathic attachment between descendants and survivors. Chapter 6 then looks at how the intergenerational transmission of trauma across a diverse set of socio-cultural factors contributes to the formation of carrier groups whose members become important social actors for the representation of the Holocaust to the wider society. In this chapter, themes of public discourse and memorialization are explored through an analysis of Holocaust commemorative events and the cultural production of Holocaust memory by descendants. Finally, the Conclusion elaborates on the social meanings of traumatic transference and the shifts in descendant representation that are taking place as the "message" of the Holocaust is being reframed through a more global and universalizing worldview.

1

Family Narratives and the Social Construction of Descendant Identity

Studies of children of Holocaust survivors have previously considered the ways in which the experiences of a traumatized parent become internalized and integrated into the psychological makeup of the child. This research emphasizes the transference of emotions, fears, and loss through conscious and unconscious processes that inform the construction of descendant identity. Beginning in 1966, psychiatric and psychological studies of first-generation descendants described children of survivors as suffering from nightmares, guilt, depression, fear of death, sadness, and the presence of intrusive images, indicators of post-traumatic stress symptoms among children of survivors (Bergman and Jucovy 1982; Prince 1985; Hass 1990; Berger 1997; Baranowsky et al. 1998; Binder-Byrnes et al. 1998; Holmes 1999). Although these symptoms have been found to vary across individual descendants, the overall findings suggest that the Holocaust, as "a dominant psychic reality" (Bergman and Jocovy 1982, 312), informs both the psychological and social development of succeeding generations. More recently, these findings have been expanded to include grandchildren of survivors (Fossion et al. 2003; Lev-Wiesel 2007).

While the psychologically based research on traumatic inheritance is extensive and ongoing, less attention has been paid to the social and cultural contexts through which knowledge of the Holocaust is learned and the impact of trauma-based knowledge on the identity formation of children and grandchildren of survivors (Danieli 2007). In particular, the role of narrative in the transmission of trauma has been somewhat neglected in studies of the Holocaust, even as the study of narrative in identity formation has become an increasingly significant mode of analysis in the social sciences. This chapter thus takes as its starting point a discussion of narrative in contemporary sociological thought. Beginning with a review of the literature on the sociology of narrative, the chapter addresses the intersection of memory and trauma narrativity in the formation of identity in the aftermath of genocide and mass trauma.

Narrative and Identity

More than two decades ago, Margaret Somers (1994) provided a theoretical framework for exploring the importance of narrative to identity formation. Challenging the notion that narratives are primarily the "telling of historical stories" (1994, 613), Somers argues that "people construct identities (however multiple and changing) by locating themselves within a repertoire of emplotted stories; that 'experience' is constituted through narrative; that people make sense of what has happened and is happening to them by attempting to assemble or in some way to integrate these happenings within one or more narratives" (1994, 614). Further, Somers suggests that is through the social networks and relationships of connectivity that narratives are given social meaning in the process of identification. In this respect, Somers suggests that identity is shaped by the narratives of events and history to which a person is connected, knowledge that is obtained through the relational interactions by which narratives are shared both publicly and within the private sphere of the family.

Following Somers, Patricia Ewick and Susan Silbey (1995) suggest that, as a form of social practice, narratives are embedded in interactions that are defined by specific social contexts which bring cultural meanings to the process of narration. Thus, narratives are cultural productions that transmit knowledge about the conditions of social life which shape the identity of both the narrator and those for whom these narratives are intended. In the case of the Holocaust, descendant identity is therefore informed by the "metanarratives" (cultural frameworks) that surround the memory of the Holocaust in society and the social networks of familial memory that preserve this history among survivors. Among the respondents in this study, it is the latter, the biographical narratives of Holocaust memory, that have been most salient for the construction of a historically situated descendant identity. Within this narrative realm of identity formation, survivor stories constitute an oral form of transmission that is distinguished from, among other narrative media, written accounts.

As a story told to another, the survivor narrative is part of the social engagement of familial relations in which survivors "narrativize experience" (Linden 1993, 18) through a recollection of events that seek to recall and give voice to what survivors and scholars alike have often deemed unrelatable. Previous research (Linden 1993; Gubkin 2007) has elaborated on the difficulty of representing the magnitude of genocidal trauma for which there is inadequate language to convey all that has been experienced and witnessed. The narratives that inform descendant identity are therefore often incomplete, a limitation that, while acknowledged, does not render these stories less meaningful for the children and grandchildren of survivors who look to these narratives for a greater understanding of the self.

The Narrator, Modes of Telling, and Tropes of Remembrance

Within this population of descendants, the role of narrator varied across and within families. In some instances it was mothers and grandmothers who spoke repeatedly about the past, while in other cases it was fathers and grandfathers who conveyed and recollected the experiences of captivity and survival. Accordingly, the transmission of memory and trauma did not reflect a gendered pattern of narration and communication, a finding that may differ from that of previous studies (Wardi 1992). In addition, in a number of cases other family members, including sisters and aunts, also acted as narrators of family history, expanding the knowledge on which participants based their descendant identity. In almost all cases, the Holocaust narration began in the descendant's childhood, although in later years narratives were sometimes revised and new accounts added, either at the request of the descendant or, more frequently, with the aging of the survivor. This was particularly true for the grandchildren of survivors, who often heard and were told stories of which their parents were unaware.

Through the interweaving of memory with historical events, the narratives of survivors provided a sense of time, place, and lived experience that became part of the knowledge and feeling-states of the descendants. According to the respondents, the survivors' accounts were characterized by a wide range of memories and trauma episodes that included descriptions of life in captivity; the living conditions of escape and imprisonment; the witnessing of other's victimization; and accounts of deportation, incarceration, and loss. The content of these narratives therefore contained "common place [sic] anchors" that, according to Ruth Linden (1993, 17), allow the descendant to interpret and understand, at least in part, the meaning of the story. As oral transmissions, these narratives were recounted in diverse social settings that included the postwar household, family gatherings, family trips, holiday celebrations, and trips to prewar homes and Holocaust memorials and museums. Two examples will help to illustrate this point. In the first, a daughter in her forties gives this account of a family dinner celebration that took place during her adolescence:

> I remember there was a restaurant that we went to, to celebrate a birthday I think. Maybe I was a teenager. It served German food. After we left there, my mother said very quietly, "I don't want to go back there. I'm pretty certain they're Nazis." She'd get this certain tone in her voice and say, "I think he [a waiter] must have been a Nazi." She and this waiter had this very curt exchange. They were very friendly and then all of a sudden something happened in the conversation and she backed way off. You could see her physically shut the door. When we were driving home, she said something about, "I'm pretty certain he had been involved in this or that." It was more like that. More like something would happen in life and

you'd get the sort of welling up of response to a situation that was more of an indication of the background behind it. There were a lot of things that would creep in.

By comparison, a fifty-five-year-old survivor offered a more contemporary perspective on the transmission of narratives among aging survivors:

> I would say in the last twenty years, [my mother] has talked about it more, but she doesn't seem to have a filter about it. So we could be sitting at the dining room table, we have a very close family. There are about fourteen of us. And we could be in the middle of a conversation, I don't know, about someone's high school graduation or an upcoming wedding, whatever the various topics would be. Everybody's just having this nice conversation and my mother will all of a sudden, something will trigger her, she'll start talking about Auschwitz. And I'll like basically freeze and want to stop it and I'll want to say, "Mom, it's not appropriate right now," and then I'm conflicted, thinking okay, well that's selfish, that I'm going into avoidance mode. This is a version of my own PTSD [posttraumatic stress disorder].

This quotation illuminates a number of important aspects of the intergenerational transmission of trauma through narrative. Both here and in the previously cited account, the interjection of Holocaust narratives into the lives of the descendants is portrayed as a random act of remembrance that was triggered by some reminder in the social environment or a conversation that may stir inner thoughts and memories of which the descendants are unaware. In both cases, the narratives that emerge from these social contexts are experienced by the descendants as intrusions into the present, bringing the survivors, their children, and grandchildren back to a past that is shared through trauma-based narrativity.

In many families, the stories were ongoing and repeated throughout the descendant's childhood and adulthood, replicating the ongoing memory frames that informed the consciousness of the survivor parent, as the following account of a sixty-year-old descendant reveals:

> My mother's stories played over and over in my mind. Sometimes she would recount the same stories, adding details as she remembered them. It always gripped me as she spoke in a sad and tearful voice; "I have to tell you," was how her stories often started. The listening sessions were not held on any regular schedule, but occurred sporadically over a fifteen-year period so I must have been six or seven when they began. The stories were realistically painted and gave me the sense that I was living through them.

Sometimes the sharing of narratives was precipitated by a parent's nightmare or sorrow, other times by actions or behaviors that mirrored the traumas of the past. A son in his late forties recounted the memories of his mother's postwar trauma activities and the narrative of camp life that engendered her behaviors:

> My mother told us about Auschwitz, how she was in Budapest in 1944 and [Adolf] Eichmann showed up and they took her away. She was there she said eighteen months and she would take things like food and other necessities and hide them in her skirts to bring to other prisoners. When I was growing up my mother collected clothes in her bedroom to send to Europe. The clothes were from the floor to the ceiling all the way around. She sent them to cousins in Hungary. At a certain point, they didn't want them any more, they didn't need them. But she kept collecting them and giving them away to people, like what she did at Auschwitz, and she couldn't stop.

As this account illuminates, survivor narratives included the retelling of events as well as the re-creation of scenes that invoked the past. A daughter thus describes how her mother reenacted an atrocity she had witnessed upon her arrival at Auschwitz: "One afternoon when retelling her stories, Mother acted out a situation where a limping woman behind her was shot by the SS guard. She showed me how the woman fell after being shot, how she cried and was left behind to bleed to death. Mother's frightening voice still rings in my ears. I can envision Mother falling to the floor, her head turned up, grimacing as she portrayed the incident." Similarly, another participant offered this recollection of her mother's performances while relating her Holocaust experiences: "She did a lot of gymnastics. She would describe standing with hand up over her head and kicking her foot up. That's my mom. She described doing this in front of the Nazis to prove how healthy she was on her own [initiative], that she was no slacker."

Based on these examples, narrative, as a link to descendant identity, involves multiple forms of communication that include both oral testimony and reenactment, each creating a social context that connects one generation's trauma to another generation's sense of self and place in the world. Although survivor narratives contain a vast array of recollections and remembrances, among the respondents in this study two competing motifs of memory were most important to identity formation: narratives that were associated with victimization and powerlessness and those that, by contrast, emphasized agency and moral choice within a culture of terror and death.

Trauma Narratives: The Imagined Victim and Identity Confusion

The stories that shape a descendant's understanding of a horrific past are often conveyed through imagery and detail that are both gripping and terrifying. In this respect, descendant generations, often at young ages, are given knowledge that lays bear the harshest and most cruel realities of war and genocide, creating both a fascination with the past and a sense of overwhelming emotion through which the descendant navigates his or her own identity and personhood. Here a son in his fifties considers how his father's narratives of the camps affected his child self:

There is no way for me to describe what it was like for me to be eight years old in my home and listen to the story of how my aunt, my father's sister, died. Because I remember him telling me that story when I was eight. And then with my Dad, it was so graphic. His memory was just incredible. He was able to remember names and faces and sights and smells. He made it real. That's all well and good, but when you are eight years old, it's a little bit much. That's the kind of atmosphere I grew up in.

For first-generation descendants (the children of survivors) in particular, their parents' narratives were steeped in memories of events and trauma that were barely a decade old. Thus, in the retelling of their experiences the closeness of the genocide heightened the sense of trauma that the narratives conveyed. Within the intimacy of the family, the lines between now and then were often blurred as the memory of atrocities traveled across time and space from Nazi Europe to the culture and consciousness of the post-Holocaust household. In addition, many of these narratives were connected to events that were taking shape in the postwar search for Nazi perpetrators, as the following account illustrates: "It was during Eichmann's trial and my mother started talking. She said, 'I saw him. He was there at the camps. I saw him. He would look into, there was this little window in the gas chamber where you could look in. I saw him looking into it and laughing. I must have been passing by, I can't remember how I saw him,' she said. 'But I absolutely saw him there.' She said he was really tall and handsome."

In a somewhat different narrative, a daughter in her fifties recalled with great detail the story her mother frequently recounted of her arrival at Auschwitz:

> One of the saddest stories my mother told me was [of] her initial arrival at Auschwitz. On the first day, she and her mother were forcibly separated, never to see each other again. Younger children were taken from their mothers and elderly women were ordered to stand with young mothers, holding their crying babies. "We pretended we didn't know why we were

separated," my mother told me, "but we put two and two together. The elderly; feeble young mothers; babies and young children [were] grouped together to be killed. My heart was torn out to see my mother in that group and I was never the same after that." My mother emphasized *never*, stressing the two syllables, and she would have a faraway look in her eyes.

Other atrocity narratives focused on acts of witnessing that took place at other death camps, at deportation sites, at places where massacres occurred, and in ghettos. In these stories, the survivor was frequently the sole member of his or her family to survive and spoke about the failure to save others whose deaths they were forced to witness. A male participant in his late forties offered this account of the knowledge that his father shared about the participant's grandfather's death at Treblinka:

> My father was all over the place. He was in the Warsaw ghetto all the way through ten different camps. He had numbers, a number. They took him to Treblinka first. They took his parents and his younger brothers to Treblinka earlier. He said from eyewitness accounts that they tested the oven there with his father and his brother. The eyewitness said, "This is what happened. They were testing the ovens. They took the son and said, 'Throw him in.' His father was standing there and he said, 'No, take me first.' The father didn't want to see the son going to his death. They said, 'No, no, you're next,' and threw him in, the son, alive and then threw the father in alive." That's one eyewitness that he knew and that he told us about, a terrible, terrible story.

It is significant to note that this survivor narrative is told through the eyes of a secondary witness whose knowledge of the family's fate shaped the atrocity stories that were handed down from father to son. Within this mode of transmission in which the survivor described in detail what he himself had not seen, the imagined horrors of the survivor converge with those of his son, whose own sense of loss and fear laid the foundation of an inherited victimized identity.

As recalled by the respondents, the atrocity narratives also revealed gender differences, with a sizeable portion focusing on fears surrounding rape and other violence against women and girls. In one example, a mother who survived Auschwitz often spoke about how Jewish women prisoners were repeatedly at risk for abuse. Here her daughter offers this insight into these gendered themes: "The story that horrified me most as a young girl was my mother's description of filing past the guards, suffering the looks, smirks, and comments exchanged among the Nazi soldiers. Because Yiddish and German are similar languages, Mother understood what was being said. 'I cowered and stooped as I walked past the guards, trying to make myself unattractive so I wouldn't be chosen for pleasure.' She noticed that a few of the prettier women had been singled out and they would disappear."

In another poignant recollection, a daughter describes how, as her father aged, he would often repeat a story about the day he witnessed the assault of his mother and sister before they were massacred:

> My father was about seventeen. He told me how they rounded up all the Jews in the village and they took them to the edge the town. As he watched, his sister and his mother were raped—and when he told this part of the story, he would stop. I don't think he would actually say the words, what he said was "They did terrible things to my mother and sister" and his eyes would well up with tears. Then he said they started shooting everyone and a few of the boys started running away and he escaped into the forest. He was the only one of his family to survive.

In one final example, a survivor chose a somewhat different approach to convey to the descendant the particular vulnerability of Jewish women. Here a fifty-five-year-old daughter describes how her survivor father used a published text as the narrative frame for Holocaust atrocity remembrance:

> We were in a used book store. He handed me this book, this used book. My dad said, "Read this." He never said that about any other book in my

life. I usually read more than he wanted me to read so it was like, this is a strange reversal. I remember specifically what the book was called. It was pornography I think. I was a little kid, eight or nine. Maybe it was about the camps. It was about this Jewish girl and what the Nazis did to her. It was all about sexual torture. Horrific. I remember the specific scene there about eyes being used as jewelry, blue eyes on Jews particularly being used in rings, and I'm thinking, "Oh my God. Why did my Dad give me this book? I have blue eyes. What was he telling me? Oh my God, what would have happened, that could be me?" This book captured so much of the stories that people were saying, so much detail and I felt so unprotected.

Taken together, both the gendered and nongendered content of atrocity narratives affects the consciousness of descendant generations in specific and important ways. It was not uncommon for participants to imagine themselves as prison inmates and, in the case of women, as rape victims, replacing the survivor in the Holocaust story. This traumatic form of identification illuminates the power of atrocity narratives to create a context through which confusion between self and other becomes possible if not inevitable (Stein 2014). Marianne Hirsch describes this phenomenon as a form of "post memory," the generational transmission of traumatic knowledge through which ". . . connection to the past is thus not actually mediated by recall but by imaginative investment, projection, and creation. To grow up with such overwhelming inherited memories, to be dominated by narratives that preceded one's birth or one's consciousness, is to risk having one's own stories and experiences displaced, even evacuated[,] by those of a previous generation" (2008, 106–7).

As Hirsch maintains, the "inherited memories" that are transmitted through family narratives provide content for both conscious and unconscious expressions of Holocaust victimhood among descendants whose dreams and fantasies place them in the traumatic landscapes of their families' past. Although this source of identification was evident in the accounts of both men and women, more women spoke about this aspect of their imagined lives. A fifty-year-old daughter explains: "[My mother] would talk about living in the barracks and makeshift soap, what they wore, how cold it was in Poland in those night shirts. And other things. I remember being five years old [and] thinking, You shouldn't be telling me this, I'm a little kid. And then you start imagining. You think the worst-case scenarios and your fantasy life starts to go hog wild and it's your mother and it's you too, we are all there together." Another daughter, also in her fifties, offered this perspective on narrative, imagination, and victimized identity: "I think the stories opened me up to being vulnerable to anything that happened. There was so much detail, gore and death. I could not tell where [my father's] life ended and mine began. It was like I was there in my imagination and my dreams."

As the foregoing accounts suggest, dreams and fantasies provide a space of imagined narrativity wherein an identification with survivor victimhood is realized through an unconscious self-construction. This dynamic was particularly true for women descendants concerning fears of rape and sexual threat, as the following example illustrates: "I used to have bad dreams. Totally about being captured, I have to tell you that I still have Holocaust dreams from time to time, about being raped, about being rounded up, about being imprisoned." While first-generation descendants were particularly vulnerable to the problems of identity confusion, atrocity narratives also played a role in the construction of identities of victimhood among grandchildren of survivors. This soical phenomenon was especially true among grandchildren who, rather than their parents, became the generational link for the narrative transmission of Holocaust trauma.

Victimized Identities among Grandchildren of Survivors

In keeping with other research, a number of grandchildren of survivors reported that they were often the one person in the family in whom the survivor confided about their past. As the survivor's confidante, the grandchild thus fulfilled the role of what Dina Wardi has described as the "memorial candle," the descendant who is chosen to preserve the personal history of the survivor and "repair the broken links" across generations (Wardi 1992, 31). A twenty-eight-year-old granddaughter who was raised in Israel in the 1990s thus describes the way in which her understanding of herself as a second-generation descendant was shaped by the narratives that her grandmother had shared with her alone:

> My grandparents didn't talk with my mom. My mom always asked a question and my grandmother was like, no no no. I am the first grandchild. My grandmother just always talked to me. We'd be sitting at the table and she'd talk with me. I knew something had happened to my grandmother. I know her face and she'd be tense and suddenly the story would jump. She was a child and then suddenly in the forest she found a little girl crying and she just took her and then suddenly after like months and months they were traveling and found her aunt and she gave the child to her aunt and she said, "I don't know if she's still alive. I don't know what happened to this little girl." And then suddenly she remembered and she would keep talking. It's like very scattered and it isn't because of her age. She's still OK. I think it's the stress of remembering.

This respondent went on to explain how, in response to her grandmother's narratives, she began to write her own Holocaust stories as a child:

> I remember when I was twelve years old there was a competition to write books. So I wrote about the Holocaust girl and I got a prize for it. There was this Holocaust girl. She lives under the bridge and the trains go over the bridge and she cut the tracks so the train falls in the water. And everybody dies, but she didn't die of course. Everybody in the train died, but at least the bad people didn't take them. I was the little girl in that story. I was totally into it.

Another granddaughter, who also grew up in Israel, was the grandchild of Jewish Polish survivors (her mother's parents). This respondent grew up on a *kibbutz* where her mother, a first-generation descendant, and her father, a Catholic, met and married in the 1960s. During her interview, she recounted stories about her survivor grandparents and the dreams of fear and victimization that have haunted her:

> I remember when I used to go with my grandmother to see her friends she would tell me if the person was a Holocaust survivor or not. It was like, be careful what you say, they are survivors. They had a number, these friends. Then I learned in increments about my own family. First, my grandfather told us that his mother died in the Holocaust and then I found out that all of his family died in the Holocaust. And then it hit home for me. This was not just something sad but a deeply personal connection. It was something I felt a very, very strong connection to always. I guess maybe I took it from them, who knows? Somehow it was in me. I was more affected by it emotionally, even among my family and my friends. I had many many nightmares on this. Until two or three years ago I can remember just being hunted by human beings, exterminated, looked for, just running away to the Swiss border, trying to pretend that I'm Christian because I have a Catholic father and his mother's prayer beads. That's one of the things where the paranoia shows up. I always travel with her prayer beads in my backpack so if anyone asks, it was like, here it is. I'm Catholic.

As an insightful case study, the life history narrative of this respondent sheds light on processes of identification that reflect fear surrounding being identified as a Jew in the world outside of Israel. Further, this participant provides other insights on identity formation especially among Israeli descendant populations. Here she offers a recollection of a children's game that she and her friends, many of whom were also grandchildren of survivors, played on the *kibbutz*:

We were a group of ten kids that were together since we were zero old. We grew up together in the same rooms. We studied together. We did everything together. So we definitely influenced each other. It was a memory I have from the fourth grade. Near our children's house there was a big ant nest, in the back of it. We decided to do a Holocaust for the ants. We called it *Shoah*. I remember the words like *Auschwitz, Nazis, Hitler* definitely tossed around. The memory is from maybe two times of year, December and the springtime. We just killed these ants, basically. It was pretty horrible when I think about it now. It was a group of us. I remember thinking, What are we doing? That it was wrong. But I went along with it. We operated like people in a group. We burned them. We built these things with matches and used matchboxes. We burned them and drowned them and smashed them. It was really horrible. It was somehow so strong in us we had to express it externally. . . . I don't even know if the ants were the Nazis or if we were the Nazis. But we treated them like the Nazis treated us, Jews. I think the most accurate thing to say was we were like the Nazis and we probably rationalized that somehow the ants were evil or mean or our enemy in some way.

In this riveting account of cross-generational identification, the participant reveals the tensions between identifying with both the victims and the aggressors of genocide. These opposing identities of powerlessness and power emerged from a childhood in which atrocity narratives shaped the selfhood of second-generation descendants whose culture and family life were influenced by the survivor community in which they were immersed beginning at young ages.

One final example of the merging of identity between second-generation descendants and their grandparents is revealed in the account of a twenty-two-year-old grandson. As part of the interview process, this young respondent (with the permission of his family) shared videos of his grandmother in which she told her life story to her grandson while being filmed by another family member. Like other grandchildren in the study, this participant, starting at a young age, was the first grandchild to whom these stories were conveyed, in part because of his deep curiosity about the past and in part because of his immersion in an educational culture that focused on the Holocaust:

> I can just remember, I guess, hearing conversation at Shabbat Friday night meals, you know it would always be a sensitive subject, and I must have been six, seven, or eight where I was the very interested kid, asking lots of questions. I was like the sponge, always gathering information. So I guess for me it was trying to learn from my grandmother and understand what she went through as a child. I was so interested in the Holocaust. I was always thinking, if I was in that position, why couldn't I escape? And then in school, I went to a private Jewish day school, and you're exposed to the Holocaust in middle school. And then I went to public school and they were talking about the story of Anne Frank. In all of this, I understood that my grandmother was in the Holocaust and I was always picturing her in those situations for sure and picturing what I would do if I were her.

This account illustrates a significant aspect of second-generation descendant identification, the intersection of family memory/narrative with that of Holocaust programming in both private and public school curricula in the United States. More so than for first-generation descendants (for whom Holocaust remembrance was not yet part of school curricula), grandchildren of survivors had a plethora of cultural narratives from which to draw that situated their grandparents in both a personal and public imaginary of terror and loss. In the case of the grandson cited previously, it was the confluence of his grandmother's narratives with those of the larger society that reinforced his imagined Holocaust identity:

> In my mind, I keep reliving what she went through, like I was there too. I know it is her story but it feels like my story too. Like my identity is

through her—a survivor of this terrible thing that happened to the Jews. And for a long time I could not stop imagining that I was also there. That's how her stories affected me. It didn't seem to affect my brothers in the same way, but some part of me feels like I went through what she went through.

Heroism, Moral Choices, and Identities of Agency

While atrocity narratives are commonly associated with descendant identification, the findings of this study also reveal the extent to which narratives of agency and empowerment affect the construction of agentic and moral identities among children and grandchildren of survivors. In this regard, the study of Holocaust memory has historically been situated in two opposing and competing narrative frames, the survivor as passive victim and the survivor as heroic actor (Langer 1991; Stein 2014). In Lawrence Langer's *Holocaust Testimonies: The Ruins of Memory* (1991), he highlights the strains in the interpretation of Holocaust narratives as either stories of heroism or painful accounts of passivity, cowardice, and traumatic numbing. Citing the work especially of Martin Gilbert, who idealizes and perhaps romanticizes the "heroism and martyrdom" (1991, 162) of those who suffered in ghettos and camps, Langer argues that "The pretense that from the wreckage of mass murder we can salvage a tribute to the victory of the human spirit is a version of Holocaust reality more necessary than true" (1991, 165). In support of his views that the Holocaust represents an unheroic rather than venerated memory, he cites the well-known work of Primo Levi and the testimonies of other survivors whose experiences of Nazi terror and dehumanization point to the loss of agency on the part of prisoners and the inability of prisoners to act on one's own or another's behalf. Ultimately, Langer concludes that survivor narratives, rather than reify the heroic, reveal the complexity of moral choices that are made by those who are rendered powerless by the conditions and inhumanity of their captivity.

In the more than two decades since Langer published his award-winning book, the questions surrounding heroism, agency, and morality during the Holocaust have continued to pervade the writings of survivors and the scholarship on genocide (Baumel 1999). As the findings of this research reveal, descendants problematize Langer's perspective and conclusions in a number of important ways that is indicative of a contemporary rethinking of the meaning of the heroic under conditions of genocidal survivorship. In this respect, the respondents challenge the notion that heroic memory is in fact a pretense, highlighting the often understated acts of heroism that their family narratives reveal. Further, in bringing their own moral interpretations to social acts during the Holocaust, the descendants focus on the survivor's agency in making difficult moral decisions. Drawing on the multiple and varied experiences that characterize survivor narratives, participants often emphasized "quiet" acts of heroism and the moral compromises that their parents and grandparents were forced to make in order to survive. Thus while they were often aware of the difficult choices of life and death that haunted a survivor's past, the respondents interpreted the moral behaviors of survivors as agentic acts that took place under unfathomable circumstances. Within this group of findings, two themes surrounding agency were most often cited as having influenced the descendants' moral identification with a parent or grandparent. The first theme is related to narratives which recall small but meaningful actions that challenge the perception of the survivor as passive and powerless. The second theme focuses on the ongoing moral dilemmas with which targeted populations are faced. While the former theme includes heroic acts among both men and women, the latter tends to center primarily on women and the moral choices surrounding acts of sexual exchange.

Narratives of Heroism and Identities of Agency

As reported by the descendants, stories of Holocaust heroism were often embedded in trauma narratives wherein terror and fear coexisted alongside acts of bravery and courage. For the participants, the heroic narrative held a special place in the telling of the family story, with descendants expressing a sense of pride at the courage of a parent or grandparent who resisted and refused to be dehumanized. These counter-narratives, which offered an alternative image of the survivor, were especially meaningful for those descendants who struggled with the fragility of a postwar traumatized parent. In the following account, a forty-eight-year-old son described the troubled mother of his childhood who, as a prisoner, helped others survive starvation at Auschwitz:

> She had nightmares and she continued not to trust any authority at all. We were all enlisted in some sort of deceptions with the government, with school, whatever it was. She had migraine headaches too and deep fears of abandonment. When she would talk about the camp, she would tell us her survival was all luck, not ever recognizing her own strength while at Auschwitz. She was there she says for about eighteen months, until the end of the war when she escaped with some other prisoners. She was a cook. As a cook, she had more access to food. But aside from what she had for herself, she hid potato skins and brought them to friends. She was noted for doing this among the camp, giving food to other people. We would ask her, "Why did you do this?" "There was nothing else to do. That is what you had to do," she said. So I learned from her these lessons about what you had to do to be a good person, even though she was deeply scarred by her experiences.

Similarly, another respondent contrasted the parent with whom he grew up—a depressed and nonresourceful father—with the storied family hero who escaped capture many times and acted with "vitality" and agency throughout the war. For this descendant, these stories provided a source of heroic identification with an otherwise ineffectual and traumatized father. Thus, the following narrative about his father's heroism deeply affected the participant's selfhood:

There's this one story that I just love. My father grew up in a schoolhouse, literally it was a schoolhouse. There was a main section and spokes off of it. Whole sections of the family would live in these different spokes. It was a huge building. It was the end of the war. The Russians had already liberated his side of Poland. My father knew that. He had been hiding and went back to his house to see who was there. All these Poles had moved in so he ran back to the Russian front and said to the Russian army, "Hey sergeant, I know a place where we all could stay, but we are going to have to kick out some Poles when we get there." So they go and kick out all the Poles knowing full well that three days later they're going to move on. So three days later, my dad runs into the woods and a day later comes back and that house became a meeting ground for all the Jewish survivors of the region. They would all come and trade notes on who saw whose family and who got killed when and where and who survived and where can I find this person and that person. It became a networking place until the Poles came back and threatened to burn the house down. I love that story. It's the vitality of my father and the resourcefulness that I rarely saw. To think, I'm going to run to the Russians knowing that they could kick them out and then I would bail when I need to. I love that story about my father.

Here a fifty-five-year-old son recalls the "strength of spirit" that emerged from his father's show of agency during the liquidation of a Polish ghetto:

There is a really famous story in the family, a really crazy story, but it actually occurred. My parents got married in the ghetto. Five months, six months later the ghetto was liquidated. Whoever was not liquidated in the ghetto went to Treblinka. You didn't get out of Treblinka. . . . There were two lines. One line was the young children, the sick, the old people, and a lot of women. It became clear to my dad that that was a bad line to be on. The other line were the young men, strong, skilled in a variety of things, and they had work cards. They were going to the line that appeared to be the staying-alive kind of line. My mom was in the wrong line. She was with her mother, two of her sisters, and some nieces and nephews. My father quickly assessed the situation. He had already gotten through. His card was stamped and he was good. He saw my mom in the wrong line and literally as she got up to the tower gate, it was a churchyard where this was going on, the SS sitting behind tables, looking at the papers, looking at the person, a stamp, you go here, you go there. My father somehow, I'm not sure of the exact way it happened, he yanked my mom off the line, literally pulled her with him right up to the table where there was an SS guy there. He literally looked at the guy and said, "She is valuable. She is a tailor, she's my wife. I want her to be in this line." I had a hard time believing that, but the part that I really had a hard time with was that he actually put his hand on the guy.

In the retelling of the story, the respondent spoke as if he were actually there, witnessing the selection in the ghetto. During his interview, he reflected on his father's quick thinking in a life-or-death situation and on the courage it took to engage in physical contact with an SS officer and defy the liquidation process. His father's narrative, which ran counter to so many images of acquiescent Jewish men, made a lasting impression on the participant, who marveled at this single act of heroism that contributed to saving his mother's life and thus made possible his own existence. Having grown up with a weakened and traumatized father, the respondent called upon this story to affirm a masculine sense of self that was identified with his father's bravery and boldness, traits of masculinity that, without the narrative, were much less apparent to the descendant. Especially for the sons of survivors, the image of the heroic father was a particularly important aspect of narrativity that framed their identification with a brave and risk-taking male parent.

Among grandchildren, similar tropes of survivor heroism were also significant for determining who they aspired to be in their own lives. A young woman, twenty-seven years of age, who was raised in Israel invoked the heroism of her grandmother, whose Holocaust memories informed much of her childhood:

These are the stories she liked repeating all the time. My grandmother was a nurse. She learned how to be a nurse. When the Germans came near their village in Poland, it was at the border of Russia and Poland. She told me that they were shooting everyone in the forest and she and my grandfather ran from the village. They were in the forest and captured a lot of times. What saved them was that my grandmother was a nurse and they needed her. It was the Russians who found them. And she told the Russians they had to take my grandfather too, [that] he could help the Russian army. The Russians needed nurses and this is how she was saved and she saved my grandfather too. I have always admired my grandmother and her stories. It's like, whoa, and I know one day I will, I will really try to be like her. She is the hero of my story too.

As the foregoing accounts demonstrate, narratives of heroism are a part of the collective memory of survivor family culture and hold a special place in the construction of the descendants' agentic identity. While these examples are in keeping with traditional notions of heroism under conditions of persecution and powerlessness, the next set of findings complicates our understanding of how gender informs agency and moral choice among victimized populations and their descendants.

Moral Identities and Sexual Exchange

The study of sexual exchange as a strategy for survival among women during the Holocaust is a relatively new area of study that reveals the way in which descendant populations adopt a nonjudgmental moral vision to the life circumstances of women's survivorship under the Nazi regime. Perhaps the first survivor to address the moral questions of women's trading sex for food and necessities was the prisoner Gisella Perl, who, as a doctor at Auschwitz, was witness both to the atrocities of the camp and the small but effective acts of agency that increased the chances of survival for women prisoners and their families. In her moving and graphic memoir, *I Was a Doctor in Auschwitz* (originally published in 1948), she speaks openly about her own troubled responses to the sex trade in which prisoners engaged. In the following excerpt from her autobiography, Perl describes the latrine (the outhouse toilets) as the center of hidden commerce within the camp grounds:

> The latrine also served as a "love nest." It was there that male and female prisoners met for a furtive moment of joyless sexual intercourse in which the body was used as a commodity with which to pay for the badly needed items the men were able to steal from the warehouses. . . . Detachments of male workers camp into Camp C almost daily, to clean the latrines, build streets, and patch up leaking roofs. These men were trusted old prisoners who knew everything there was to know about camp life, had connections in the crematoria, and were masters at "organizing." Their full pockets made them the Don Juans of Camp C. They chose their women among the youngest, the prettiest, the least emaciated prisoners and in a few seconds the deal was closed. . . . At first I was deeply ashamed at these practices. My pride, my integrity as a woman revolted against the very idea. . . . But later, when I saw that the pieces of bread thus earned saved lives, when I met a young girl with shoes, earned in a week of prostitution, saved her from being thrown into the crematory, I began to understand——and forgive. (1993, 112–13)

Although Perl's writings are more than sixty years old, it was not until Joan Ringelheim's (1997) pathbreaking essay on genocide and gender that the questions surrounding sexual exchange and rape were directly addressed within the study of women's experiences during the Holocaust. In this work, Ringelheim highlights the silence around these gendered aspects of survival and her own discomfort in interviewing women who had been sexually abused: "The impulse to neutralize the issue of sex by treating it as non-existent or insignificant is entirely understandable. The possible rape of mothers, grandmothers, sisters, friends, or lovers during the Holocaust is difficult to face. The further possibility that mothers or sisters or lovers 'voluntarily' used sex for food or protection is equally difficult to absorb. All the experiences connected to sex, whether negative or positive, are understandably troublesome" (1997, 25). While Ringelheim is careful to point out that the "Holocaust is not about sex" (1997, 25), her work is a reminder that women were sexually exploited and that their survival often depended, as Perl observed, on trading sex for food and lifesaving commodities. Following Ringelheim, the importance of sexual bartering during the Holocaust has most recently been explored in a study of ghetto society in Theresienstadt, where the practice of trading sex for survival needs was not uncommon (Hajkova 2013). In bringing a feminist perspective to this study, Anna Hajkova argues that, given the power relations of ghetto society in which male prisoners had control over women's lives, instrumental sex "improved women's positions, thereby strengthening their sense of agency" (2013, 23).

In an interesting and significant finding of this study, a number of descendants similarly acknowledged the reality and importance of sexual bartering as an act of agency that they understood and with which they could identify, given the constraints of prisoner society. Among these respondents, mothers and grandmothers were typically described as "beautiful" women whose sexuality undoubtedly played a role in their ability to survive, as one son maintained: "My mother was in Auschwitz. She told me she was never sexually approached, which I have a hard time believing because she was a really good-looking woman. Things happen and things don't happen. One of the things that I've grown to appreciate is that each person's survival story is so unique. They are made up of very individual stories. Her story is one of amazement that she survived."

While this account, like many others, relies on inference and assumptions about women's sexuality and survivorship, other accounts are more explicit in reporting acts of sexual exchange. In this regard, descendants describe a range of sexual relationships in which their mothers and grandmothers engaged, including those with other prisoners, Nazi officials, and non-Jews who were in a position to help a survivor in captivity, as an escapee or during liberation. In retelling these stories, respondents distinguished between rape and sexual bartering, often quick to point out that such exchanges were among the few options available to women who sought to protect themselves and others from harm. As such, rather than a moral failure of a powerless victim, these exchanges were represented as pragmatic and agentic responses to the power relations of prisoner culture. A daughter in her fifties thus described her mother as a role model for using both her wits and her sexuality to survive Auschwitz:

> I'll give you another very interesting sidelight. My mother never lost her periods during Auschwitz. As I said, this woman is very sharp. She was able to get herself a day job inside instead of toiling in the fields. I think she was seventeen years old. There she was a pipsqueak of a girl. She was empowered, she was surviving. She was beautiful and I know there is much more to the story than meets the eye. There were hints, more than hints sometimes, that she was somebody's mistress. And she always taught my sister and me that being beautiful, looking well dressed, is really important, no matter how poor or in need you are.

Although this respondent reported that she sometimes imagined the "worst case scenarios" for her mother in the camp, she also saw her mother as a model of strength whose choice to use sexual bartering offered an alternative identification to the totally passive death camp victim.

In another example, that of a grandmother who was believed to have used sexual bartering to protect herself and her young daughter, a grandson in his thirties explains how his moral selfhood emerged out of his grandmother's experience:

> My grandmother, although she didn't want to talk about it, was the most survival oriented. I don't know that I want to know everything that she had to do so survive. There were a lot of interesting friendships with men

along the way. I wouldn't be surprised to hear that some of them were more than friendships. I have been very blunt with my mother, asking her, "Do you think she traded sexual favors?" [My mother] said to me, "You know I have thought about this and I think it's possible in cases A and B and I really don't think it happened in cases C and D." I don't really know for sure, but I have suspicions. There are choices that people had to make to survive. I don't judge. To be lowered to a position of complete subordination and having to negotiate somehow. I have information from the stories I've heard. And it has made me a different person, not to judge others if you don't know what they have been through. [My grandmother] and I were very close and she is a model for me of a certain type of strength and will to survive.

In what might be considered a significant "moral turn," descendants are not only defining survivorship itself as a form of agency, but they are also acknowledging the strong possibility that sexual bartering may have been key to their mothers' and grandmothers' ability to support themselves and others. Among the respondents in this study, these narratives have helped to shape a more nuanced moral perspective among succeeding generations who express an understanding of the complex moral choices that women survivors were forced to make. Given Ringelheim's earlier observations, what is perhaps most surprising about the participants' discourse on sexual exchange is the openness with which they discussed the survivor's imagined or confirmed liaisons, explaining that these gendered social behaviors were normative given the social conditions under which the women survived. For the descendants, the narratives concerning women's sexuality during the Holocaust not only inferred the violence of sexual abuse and rape but also allowed for a more empowered interpretation of women's agency in which sexual exchanges and bartering were among the few instrumental acts of survivorship in which women could and did engage.

Overall, the findings in this chapter reveal the importance of Holocaust narratives for the construction of the descendant self. In returning to the work of Somers (1994), the research confirms that past events that are embedded in traumatic narration provide an important path to the development of social identities across generations. As survivors conveyed their personal histories to their children and grandchildren, the narrative content of their stories helped to shape the self-concepts of the descendants concerning notions of victimhood, agency, and gendered norms and expectations. The value of oral narrative for the transference of trauma is thus one significant dynamic of traumatic inheritance. A second, equally significant aspect of Holocaust transmission is ritual practices within the family. These practices, which rely on emotional transference rather than on narrative storytelling as the medium for traumatic exchanges, are examined in the chapter that follows.

2

Ritual and the Emotional Transmission of Holocaust Trauma

The research on the intergenerational transmission of trauma focuses primarily on two modes of survivor communication: storytelling, as discussed in the previous chapter, and deep emotional silences (Baranowsky et al. 1998) that convey what Dan Bar-On (1995) has termed "the untold story," feelings and emotions that permeated the emotional climate of the survivor household. According to Bar-On, it was these unspoken feelings that were often most influential in the emotional transference of Holocaust trauma. The findings of this study suggest that in addition to spoken narratives and emotional silences, the trauma of the Holocaust was also transmitted through ritual practices and family traditions that elicited deep feelings on the part of survivors, creating a space of emotional memory that connected both the survivor and the descendant to the traumatic past. Turning first to a discussion of the function of ritual in the intergenerational transmission of trauma, this chapter will consider ritual as a site of emotional exchange, as a vehicle for socioemotional distancing among descendants, and as an emotion-based link both to Jewish heritage and to the survivor generation. With regard to the last theme, the chapter will explore the role of ritual and emotion among members of descendant populations who were raised in the United States as well as those who were raised in eastern Europe.

Ritual as a Site of Posttraumatic Emotion

In the study of ritual and emotion, the work of Durkheim (2001) and Clifford Geertz (1973) elaborates the ways in which group rituals are the site of shared emotions that connect group members to an ancestral past. As a source of cohesion and memory, rituals thus provide a means by which group identity is formed and sustained among individuals with a common history and shared culture. Scholars such as Thomas Scheff (1979) and Victor Turner (1969) further examine the emotional character of ritual performance that allows participants to express and externalize repressed feeling-states, creating conditions under which the cathartic release of emotion is made possible. Following these theorists, Frederick Bird (1995) has explored the ways in which religious ritual functions particularly in the family, outlining four dimensions of family-based ritual practice. Among these dimensions are the expression of feelings that ordinarily are silenced in the family and the affirmation of cultural identity through the maintenance of religious traditions. These interrelated functions of family ritual, as articulated by Bird, were found to be especially significant in the post-Holocaust family. Accordingly, familial ritual practice became an important site for the cross-generational transmission of trauma.

Turning to the study of posttraumatic stress disorder among survivor populations, Judith Herman (1992) describes a cycle of emotional repression and expression in which survivors vacillate between remembering and forgetting, a contradictory set of responses that results in a "dialectic of trauma" (1992, 50) in which states of rage, hatred, and grief alternate with periods of numbness and emotional disconnection. According to the accounts of the children of survivors, the cycle of expression became embedded in the ritual performances of their parents, who, through religious practice and traditions, relived the emotions of their traumatic past. In particular, the participants reported that the observance of Yom Kippur (the Day of Atonement), the holiest day of the Jewish year, was especially significant for the evocation of traumatic memory and the attending expression of traumatic feelings in the survivor household. As described in the descendant narratives, the observance of this religious holiday was recalled as a time of great emotional strain within the family, as feelings of anger, guilt, and inconsolable sadness permeated the emotional dynamics of fasting and prayer. Aaron Hass, a scholar of

Holocaust trauma and a first generation descendant, describes the Yom Kippur ritualization of his father's Holocaust narrative in this way:

> The ritual began when I was eight or nine years old and lasted for about ten years. It took place on the night of Yom Kippur. In observance of Jewish legal restrictions, our apartment in Brooklyn was dark except for a shaft of light coming from under the closed door of the bathroom. This streak would be our lantern in the blackness. One was not permitted to switch on electricity for twenty-four hours during this holy period.
>
> The story was brief and always the same. The somber environment and the mystical day on which it was told lent an eeriness to the account. We lay on my parents' bed, my father lying on his side, I on my right side facing him. I could barely make out the outlines of his face. My father spoke in Yiddish. "We [the partisans] found out that a German officer would be at the farmhouse of a Pole who had betrayed Jews to him. The German was probably delivering two bottles of vodka as payment for the two Jews the Pole handed over. We came in and they were drinking together. We tied them up and cut a small hole in each one's arm. For hours we put salt in the open wounds. Then we shot them both."
>
> My father's voice reflected an increasing bitterness as the story progressed. I absorbed my father's determination as he spoke, and I felt my anger swell. I was fascinated. I was also frightened. (Hass 1990, 68–69)

In this autobiographical account, Hass captures the feeling states that were aroused during his father's ritual storytelling in the "eerie" atmosphere of Yom Kippur. In this example, the narrative structure of storytelling, as described in chapter 2, is embedded in a ritualized recitation that defines the meaning of Yom Kippur for the descendant. In a complex ritual of religious observance that blends atrocity narration with strong emotional expression, Hass internalized both the anger of the perpetrator/father as well the fear of a young child who became witness to the scene of his father's rage and violence. As this case powerfully illustrates, the observance of the High Holy Days was framed by emotion-laden memories that were relived each year on Yom Kippur. Further, in Hass's recollection, it is the father who symbolizes the rage and violence of the perpetrators while it is the German officer and the Polish informants who are remembered as the victims of torture and terror.

Like Hass, a number of respondents in this study also spoke of ritual as a site of emotional transference concerning Holocaust memories. These accounts, however, differed from Hass's experience in that the emotion-based rituals were more frequently enacted without an accompanying narrative, the ritual itself invested with the anger, pain, and despair that signified the emotional legacy of a traumatic past. In this respect, the observance of the High Holy Days, and especially Yom Kippur, was marked by strong emotions that were directed primarily at God. Torn between moral outrage at a god who had let so many innocent Jews die and a deep moral commitment to keep Judaism alive, the survivors conveyed a complicated set of emotions that were brought on especially by the period of reflection and repentance that the holiday demanded. In the following account, a fifty-two-year-old participant who was raised in an Orthodox Jewish home describes how his father's rage toward God became intertwined with the family's adherence to religious tradition:

> My Dad was raised by a very, the word he uses, is "pious" man. His father was extremely religious. He came from a large family. It was a very rigid reality. This is what life is about, studying Talmud and the Torah. It was really jammed down his throat. Then his dad, my grandfather, was taken away and murdered and the rest of the family was killed. My father and his brother were the only survivors. When he started to raise his own family, he was still coming from this place of guilt and anger. . . . I had to be bar mitzvahed—there was no choice—we had to keep kosher, keep the Sabbath, fast, light candles, and if my mother showed up at things without her wig, that was like heresy. But Yom Kippur? That was always the

hardest, when the anger and bitterness [were] the strongest—it was just a kind of jammed down your throat—[a] "this is the way it is" kind of thing without any depth. The only feelings were [those] of rage and bitterness.

As these two narratives illustrate, the observance of Yom Kippur became associated with the remembrance of violence and rage in one case, and the transmission of embittered feelings toward God in the other case. Although these accounts each offer a different perspective on the effects of anger in the intergenerational transference of trauma, both reveal the important role that the Yom Kippur ritual played in engendering memories of a specifically Jewish trauma and the posttraumatic feeling-states that such memories evoke.

A second and equally powerful set of emotions that were triggered by the observance of the Day of Atonement were those feelings associated with survivor guilt. Because Yom Kippur is a day of atonement, the liturgy for this religious holiday involves the recitation of sins for which the supplicant asks God for forgiveness and mercy. As research on survivors has poignantly shown, the memory of survivorship was often accompanied by feelings of self-blame and guilt that, in the aftermath of catastrophe, contributed to the posttraumatic symptoms of the surviving generations (Langer 1991; Herman 1992). It is thus not surprising that Yom Kippur, with its emphasis on sin and self-recrimination, was a difficult and angst-ridden holiday in the survivor family.

The narrative of a woman respondent will help to illustrate this dimension of the High Holy Days observance. Piecing together her mother's war-time experiences from stories that she was told as a young child, the respondent, now in her fifties, recounted how her mother was deported at age seventeen to Auschwitz, where she survived by working in a munitions factory. The respondent said that although her mother spoke with pride of her survival, there was an unspoken subtext to her stories, an undercurrent of silence, regret, and guilt that surfaced especially during her observance of Yom Kippur:

Surviving such a horrendous event, you can't begrudge anybody for doing what they had to do to get by at Auschwitz. My mother suffers from survivor guilt. Because there is another side of the story. Remember I told you there were nine siblings, including my own mother? I believe it was 1941, her mother and father went to some little town near Krakow where they were hiding. It was a tiny little village. My mother was in Krakow at that time and she heard that they were going to the village to kill all the Jews. She was able to get to a telephone and she called but there was no answer. She knew right then and there that that was it for her parents. Then her uncles, their children, her little nieces with whom she was very close—all killed. . . .

My mother did not want to raise us Jewish. We were Unitarians. I think that being Jewish was too painful. Having said that, [I can say that] she observed all the holidays. We had Passover, and Yom Kippur was very sad for her. She would gorge herself the day before so that she could spend the whole day fasting. . . . She would just lie in bed all day. My sister and I were scared because it was the one time a year when her feelings of guilt and grief overwhelmed her and she couldn't eat or move or even talk to us. There was just this silence and her pain.

As this account reveals, even in nonreligious Jewish households survivors observed the Yom Kippur ritual, maintaining a yearly tradition in which painful emotions were given expression and visibility in the postcatastrophe culture of the survivor family.

Along with fasting and the recalling of sins and wrongdoing, it is traditional on Yom Kippur to remember family members who have died. At the onset of the holiday, the lighting of memorial (*yahrzeit*) candles in the home signals the beginning of a memorial period. Accordingly, the participants in this study gave vivid and emotional accounts of kitchen countertops and dining room tables that were lined with ritual candles, small glass containers with Hebrew lettering that, for the children of survivors, came to symbolize the Jewish nature of traumatic loss. A woman in her sixties whose father died when she was twelve recounted an early childhood memory when her father's only connection to Judaism was framed through this act of memorialization:

> My father escaped deportation, jumped the train, and came to [...]. It is unclear whether his parents died in Theresienstadt or Auschwitz. My father grew up Jewish. My grandmother, my father's mother, was Orthodox and when he married my mother everyone said she was a foreign woman, even though she was a Jew, because she came from [...]. My mother did not keep a kosher home and was not brought up in a religious home. After the war, my father was not religious but he kept Yom Kippur and Rosh Hashanah and he always lit a *yahrzeit* candle for his father. That was very important to me—the only time I would see his grief when his feelings were not hidden. I remember I talked to him about it and how important it was. And I light a *yahrzeit* candle for him every year. I feel I owe it to him.

Grandchildren also recalled the memorialization of lost family members during the High Holy Days period, remarking that as young children it was often the first recognition and awareness of the solemnity of the day and the memory of death that permeated the observance of this ritual. As one granddaughter explained, candles were the signifier of her grandparents' loss and of deep sadness: "It's strange but my connection to it all is all about the candles. The Yom Kippur candles and the Holocaust."

In addition to memorials candles, this holiday also evoked other ritual practices that in some cases were outside the norm of religious observance within the family and which affected both children and grandchildren of survivors. Here a twenty-eight-year-old granddaughter recounts a transformative ritual event that her mother observed when the respondent was still an infant and that she passed on to her daughter through an emotionally charged recollection of the ritual scene:

My grandfather lost most of his affiliation with religion, although the one story I have been told by my mom about him is [from] when I was still a baby. My grandparents lived on the bottom level and my parents lived on the middle level and my aunt and uncle lived on the top level of a tri-story building. So my mom would always drop me off with my grandfather for babysitting. She would just come in and drop me off and go, without any scheduling or notice. He had lost both his legs and here he is in a wheelchair and he is not going anywhere. They had a long sofa like they did back in those days, with a coffee table in front. I would run to one end of the sofa, or crawl over there—I wasn't walking yet—and hold out my hands and make motions that I wanted him to pick me up. So anyway, [my mother] would drop me off to play games with my grandfather. One day she walked in unannounced and he was davening. It must have been around the holiday. He had his *tallis* [prayer shawl] over his head, draped over the back of the wheelchair, and he had *tefillin* [ritual objects] on his head and his arms. She had never seen that before. It made such an impression on her, the *tefillin* wrapped around his tattoo on his forearm, that that vision just stuck with her for her whole life. I think it is one of those moments when you come in on such a personal moment that you can't even speak about it. The story ends with her seeing him.

This narrative has many important elements that underlie the transference of trauma across generations. First, while the respondent is central to the ritual event, it is her mother's passing on of the memory that situates the infant respondent within her grandfather's ritual act, the meaning and feelings of which cannot adequately be conveyed with words. Second, the trauma of the ritual witnessing is associated with the juxtaposition of religious artifacts against the tattooed and disabled body of the survivor. Thus, the transference of trauma takes place within the imaginary of the descendant where emotion and ritual observance converge around the recollection of embodied victimization.

While Yom Kippur and the attending High Holy Days were remembered as the most emotion-laden rituals in survivor households, the participants also reported other forms of observance that left a deep impression on descendants. Surrounded by a culture of sadness, loss, and anger, the respondents frequently described their ritual lives as joyless, rigid, and obligatory. A number of respondents remarked on the rigidity with which their families kept kosher, observed the Sabbath, or strictly maintained the dietary rules of Passover, their parents becoming angry or upset if a rule or law was violated. Others remarked on the compulsive and often depressing observance of holidays such as Sukkoth (the Feast of the Tabernacles) that, while for other Jews was celebratory and festive, for their families were unhappy and despairing occasions: "My parents didn't take particular joy in practicing ritual. They felt that this was the way they were brought up and they didn't want us to lose the identity. I remember hating Sukkoth because we never did anything joyful or exciting. My father didn't go to work. We didn't go to school but there was no warmth, no bringing us together, just the persistent memory of who was not there, who would not be celebrating with us."

The findings on the persistence of Jewish rituals among observant as well as non-observant survivors suggest that, in the aftermath of the Holocaust, ritual practice was one means by which the emotional trauma of the catastrophe was conveyed to the next generation. Along with the telling of atrocity narratives and/or the feeling-laden silences that were pervasive in the postwar family culture, the practice of ritual established a separate but compelling emotional space wherein descendants were witness to the survivors' suffering and rage and wherein the emotional boundaries across generations, especially between survivors and the first generation of descendants, became blurred within a ritualized context of Jewish observance. Thus, as an important site of emotional exchange, the significance of ritual for the intergenerational transmission of trauma can in part be explained through the paradigm of self-in-relation theory.

Ritual as a Site of Emotional Exchange: Self-in-Relation Theory and the Cross-Generational Transmission of Trauma

In the past decade, scholars have put forward various theoretical models to explain the relationship between the intergenerational transmission of trauma and personality development among children of survivors. Within this field of study, Natan Kellerman (2001d) identifies four models of transmission that have come to dominate the literature on the first-generation descendants: psychoanalytic, social learning, communication, and relational theory. The psychoanalytic view suggests that the child "unconsciously absorbs the repressed and insufficiently worked-through Holocaust experiences of survivor parents" (Kellerman 2001d, 260). The social learning and family system theories focus on the more overt ways in which survivor parents engaged in inadequate or destructive parenting behaviors while establishing closed family systems in which the interdependency between the child and the parent created an obstacle to the child's independence. And last, the relational model, based on object relations theory, emphasizes a psychodynamic in which the child internalizes the traumatized parent, who then becomes a reflection of the child self (Holmes 1999).

Expanding on Kellerman's discussion, a fifth model of transmission, the self-in-relation perspective (Chodorow 1978; Jordan et al. 1991), can add further insight on the child's identification with a traumatized parent. Originating from the relational school of development, the self-in-relation paradigm takes as its starting point the exchange of feelings that, beginning in infancy, takes place between the child and caregiver. As such, this theory shifts the emphasis in development from the internalization of a parent-object to the emotional relationship that characterizes the parent–child dynamic. Feminist in orientation, self-in-relation theory highlights the value of empathy (the emotional identification with the feelings of others) in personality development and illuminates the way in which identity evolves from the strong emotional connection that takes place between a parent and child, as articulated in the work of Jean Baker Miller: "The earliest representation of the self, then, is of a self whose core—which is emotional—is attended to by other(s) and in turn, begins to attend to the emotions of other(s). Part of the internal image of oneself includes feeling the other's emotions and acting on them as they are in interplay with one's own emotions" (Miller 1991, 14).

Beginning with the work of Miller (1991; 1996) and Nancy Chodorow (1978), the relational paradigm emerged in response to the male-centered models of psycho-social maturation that highlighted the importance of separateness, individuation, and autonomy for healthy transitions into adulthood. In challenging the traditional psycho-social models of development, in which girls, because of their connectivity, were consistently represented as less mature, less developed, and less moral than boys, feminist scholars sought to reinterpret the connective aspects of development, showing that connectivity enhances rather than undermines a girl's sense of self. Over the past three decades, the self-in-relation school has produced a plethora of scholarship that has reframed child and adolescent development through the values of connection and attachment. Central to this theoretical model is the role that empathic attachment plays in a girl's relational world, and especially the importance of the mother–daughter bond:

> Here we are describing the girl's open relationship with the mother and the mother's open relationship with the daughter as the beginning stage for the development of the self-in-relation. The second key aspect of this relationship is the child's increasing capacity for mutual empathy, developed in a matrix of emotional connectedness. . . . Through the girl's awareness and identification with her mother as the "mothering one" and through the mother's interest in being understood and cared for, the daughter as well as the mother becomes mobilized to care for, respond to, or attend to the well-being and development of the other. (Surrey 1991, 56)

In applying the self-in-relation model to the findings on ritual and the transference of trauma, the findings suggest that under conditions of traumatic transmission, young boys as well as young girls develop an empathic attachment to the survivor parent. This developmental phenomenon demonstrates that the emotional exchange between parent and child is informed not only by gender but also by the social conditions that affect feeling-states within the family, especially in posttraumatic cultures. In this respect, the narratives of the respondents indicate that the practice of ritual provided a familial space wherein the emotional boundaries between parent and child were especially permeable. As a site of emotional transference, ritual thus played a significant role in establishing a relational environment that fostered, through empathy and connectivity, the child's emotional identification with a traumatized parent. While women respondents were perhaps affected more strongly by ritualized exchanges, both men and women in the study describe themselves as having emotionally "absorbed" the trauma of their parents. Here a female respondent, now in her fifties, describes this internalization of her parents' suffering: "As a young child, what I lived was the emotional pain in my body that I was receiving from them. Children pick up everything. My parents lived in so much grief. How can you even imagine them emotionally surviving all that suffering? I intuited the pain that they lived in and that was in their bodies. I didn't know how to separate myself from it." As this account illustrates, children of survivors express shared feelings for their parents' trauma that, in part, can be explained by the transfer of emotion that took place during ritual observances in the survivor household. Ritual therefore provided a social context for enhancing and reinforcing the confusion between self and other that was described in the previous chapter. Much of the earlier research on first-generation descendants addresses this problem of enmeshment among children of survivors (Sorscher and Cohen 1997; Fonagy 1999; Kellerman 2001d). More recently, studies of grandchildren have also shown some similar patterns of boundary confusion. Because of the centrality of ritual to emotional enmeshment, both children and grandchildren of survivors have turned to ritual innovation as a pathway for establishing a separate sense of self within a cultural framework that sustains links both to the survivor generation and to the descendant's Jewish heritage.

Forging Separate Identities: Culture-Bearing and the Reinvention of Jewish Ritual among Descendants

The data from this study strongly support the finding that while ritual was a site of emotional exchange in the formative years of descendant development, in adulthood the practice of ritual facilitated a process of separation and individuation. Over the past decade, research in the sociology of religion has pointed to a number of significant trends in religion and spirituality among the Baby Boomer generation. Among these trends, documented by scholars such as Wade Clark Roof (1999) and Robert Wuthnow (1998), is a decisive move toward religious creativity, individualism, and ritual invention. Like others of their generation who came of age in the cultural dislocations of the 1960s, the children of Holocaust survivors embraced the values of religious experimentation and innovation as they sought to negotiate the difficult emotional terrain of their descendant upbringing. Although the innovative strategies of the respondents look somewhat similar to those of their nondescendant counterparts, the social-psychological lens through which the children of survivors sought out ritual innovation was distinctly different. As one respondent remarked, "As a child of survivors, you feel this obligation to make sure Hitler doesn't succeed. At the same time, you don't want to do it the way your parents did—you want holidays to be fun, to bring joy. So I think you have to do more than just observe the rituals—you have to do it differently."

Faced with a moral obligation to preserve Judaism and a competing psychological need to separate from their traumatized Jewish parents, the children of survivors created new ritual forms that maintained Jewish tradition without reproducing the traumatizing ritual experiences of their childhood. Rejecting the sadness, grief, and rage of the survivor culture, the adult children of survivors intentionally and self-consciously reinvented Jewish customs in a manner that strongly differentiated their observance from that of their parents. Not surprisingly, among the rituals that were of particular importance to the project of creative innovation were those that focused on Yom Kippur. Given the significance of the Day of Atonement for survivors, the majority of respondents sought ways to bring new meaning to a holy day that had deep associations with parental despair. A nonpracticing male participant in his forties thus described the alternative ritual he created for the observance of this holiday:

> We don't do the High [Holy Days]. I just can't resonate with them. I guess I am somewhat rebellious around Yom Kippur in particular, about fasting on that day. Yet, being the son of somebody who is a Holocaust survivor, it is hard for me to just ignore the traditions. There are times when I go off on my own for two or three days on a kind of vision quest. I'll sit with myself and not eat and I try to think about what Yom Kippur is designed to do—what it is all about—what does it mean to repent when you have this terrible history.

This innovative approach to Yom Kippur is also found among numerous other Jews in the United States who are seeking to create new ritual practices that incorporate meditation and prayer in natural and non-institutionalized settings (Eisen 1998). For the first generation of descendants such alternatives have great appeal in part because they offer nontraditional modes of spiritual reflection that are far removed from the overwhelming emotional experiences that their parents had conveyed during High Holy Days observance. In an interesting and important development, similar themes of reflection and spirituality are also found among second-generation descendants. Here a granddaughter of survivors who practices Buddhism describes the meaning with which she approaches Yom Kippur each year: "I don't go to services on any other occasion than Yom Kippur. And Yom Kippur feels right to do that. [There] is always something pretty magical about being in synagogue, even though I don't follow the prayers or the rules. It is the notion of being in community and feeling my spirituality in that space."

While new approaches to Yom Kippur were among the most solemn and serious of the ritual innovations, the reinvention of ritual among the respondents also included other customs, most notably those that were associated with the traditions of the Sabbath and Passover. Surveys of Jews in the United States suggest that a little over a quarter of the Jewish population regularly prepares a traditional Friday night dinner to usher in the beginning of the Sabbath (Saxe et al. 2006). Among the respondents in this study, nearly one-third of them routinely maintained Friday night dinners as a means to foster a family culture of connection and relatedness. Here an unaffiliated woman respondent offers this view of the weekly Sabbath customs that she practices in her home:

> I don't consider myself religiously Jewish at all. But I definitely practice the Jewish rituals. I made a chalice that I use for Friday night when we light the candles and say the blessings over the wine. We always have Friday night dinner. Our daughter thinks *challah* is the best food substance in the land. But Friday night candles are the most important ones for me. [This practice] keeps my relationship with my parents and yet because we do it so differently—with our own prayers and blessings and family time—it is our own.

Similarly, another respondent, also a mother, recast the melancholy Sabbath observance of her childhood through a lens of connection to family and friends: "The kids wouldn't give up Friday night for anything. It's the only time [when] we sit down together. It's a very special night for them. When we were kids, it was so different. It was just us with our parents. They were so busy trying to get life together [that] there was no time for us really—not even on the Sabbath. Now we have our kids and our friends and we all get together and share the week with one another."

In both of these accounts, the Sabbath, especially Friday night dinner, was maintained as a ritual of connectedness through which Jewish identity was reshaped and sustained. The traditional concepts that mark the Sabbath as a liminal space that separates the sacred from the profane were thus replaced with meaning systems that emphasized familial continuity and cultural connection. This phenomenon, which has also been documented in other research on Jewish women and tradition (Davidman 1991), was especially pronounced among daughters of survivors who tended to focus on the relational value of ritual rather than the importance of Jewish law for Sabbath observance.

Among the grandchildren, alternative Sabbath observance was also reported by the participants, especially those who grew up within an extended family culture wherein a survivor grandparent rigidly adhered to and enforced Orthodox practices. In the following account, a twenty-two-year-old grandson whose grandmother had survived Auschwitz and Bergen-Belsen describes his efforts to keep the Sabbath while distancing himself from his grandmother's traditional demands, such as the prohibition on driving on the Sabbath:

> How I lived growing up was kind of hiding out sometimes. We would have Friday night dinner at my grandmother's and I would drive when I got older but I would pull the car around the block, this is how ridiculous I get, I would pull the car around and walk over and I'll walk back. I still do it when I go home. But that is not how I live here when I am away from home. Here I pray a little every day just for myself. I try to have Shabbat dinner with my friends and we are just hanging out with each [other], sharing a meal, lighting candles, eating *challah*, and drinking wine.

The celebration of Passover offered yet another ritual context for innovation and creativity. Here, more than in any other ritual observance, the participants linked the remembrance of Jewish catastrophe with a moral imperative to move beyond an explicitly Jewish worldview, as one respondent explained:

The holiday that we do in our hearts is Passover. We try to be inclusive [then]. We try to go beyond the concept of the slavery of Jews. When I was growing up, my family was always about us and them [Jews and non-Jews]. That's what my family has always been about, us and them. So I try to be inclusive and open the idea up to the concept of slavery that we have in our world, in our hearts, ourselves, the prisons that we create for ourselves. In that way, we don't hide that it comes from a Jewish thing; we talk about it. In that way, we bring in some Jewish holidays but with a more universal understanding.

Significantly, Passover provided a ritual context for the descendant's shift from the "us and them" mentality that fueled the fears and anxieties of the survivor generation. Because the story of the Jews' enslavement in Egypt can be read as a timeless parable of resistance and empowerment, Passover became a valuable form of ritual observance for many of the respondents. In seeking to resolve the tensions between a longing to remain connected to Jewish heritage and the need to distance themselves from the trauma of their parents and grandparents, the story of the liberation of the Jews from Egypt was reinterpreted through a more contemporary perspective on enslavement and oppression, an approach to the holiday that separated the descendants from a more problematic ritualized past. In expanding the notion of human suffering beyond the boundaries of Jewish experience, the children and grandchildren of survivors found ways to incorporate values of social justice into their ritual lives, an innovation that, in making a break from the family tradition, helped to define an individual and separate identity.

Last, for those participants who do not consider themselves to be religiously Jewish, among the rituals that were most important were those that bestowed upon their children the "right" of Jewish heritage. One respondent, currently a member of the Unitarian community, expressed great concern that her adopted child would not be considered Jewish unless she underwent a traditional conversion ceremony that included immersion in a *mikveh* (ritual bath). She thus sought out a rabbi who would perform this rite with her young daughter:

> We were determined to have my daughter be Jewish and to take her to the *mikveh*. We tried. At the very last moment my daughter broke her leg and she had a stress fracture, so she had a brace on. The rabbi in all of her wonderfulness said she couldn't go into the *mikveh* because the *mikveh* had to touch all of her body parts. I thought she was joking initially, and she wasn't. She was very fundamentalist around this process. So at the very last moment, we went to a friend's swimming pool and we gave her Mogen David wine and we had *challah* and we sang. The swimming pool was the *mikveh*. She had been practicing how to jump in before the day and so she just jumped in. So she is Jewish and "they" can deal with it later.

This account is especially informative because it highlights two significant qualities of first-generation descendants: the desire to ensure the Jewishness of their children, regardless of their religious orientation; and their willingness to create new rituals when the traditional approach fails. In this telling narrative, the alternative *mikveh* rite, while a departure from traditional Jewish law, nevertheless met the individual criteria of the respondent whose openness and flexibility were characteristic of other descendants who prided themselves on their creativity and their ability to distance themselves from the more painful aspects of the survivors' ritual lives. Although ritual is only one means by which descendants seek to unravel the deep and often troubling emotional connections to the suffering of survivors, the example of the adaptive *mikveh* rite highlights the kinds of creative resolutions that succeeding generations have developed in response to the conflicting emotional needs that have framed the life experiences of children and grandchildren of survivors.

Ritual Practices and Culture-Bearing among Descendants

As the foregoing analysis suggests, the practice and creation of ritual contributes to an autonomous descendant identity. Through the practice of ritual innovation, descendants honor a religious ancestry that is steeped in the memory of genocide while finding pathways to separation and individuation from the trauma of survivor culture. In this way, ritual observance, even among the innovators, represents a trend toward culture-bearing that is found more generally among descendants. This trend was particularly significant among grandchildren of survivors who sought to maintain a connection to an aging or deceased grandparent through the maintenance of traditions that had been of importance to the survivor generation. Here a granddaughter in her late twenties describes her observance of Chanukkah: "I always want to do Chanukkah. And I'm so not religious. When I went to a retreat, I did Chanukkah. There were some other Jews there but I was the only person who was like, 'I want to do Chanukkah.' It was so strange—among 150 people, we were three Jews including myself. The people that ran the retreat were more than happy to facilitate with everything. It's different being Jewish for me. The others were coming from a very different place than [I]."

For other grandchildren, observing Passover represented a connection to both Jewish culture and to a survivor with whom the descendant shared a special relationship. A thirty-two-year-old female respondent offered this perspective on the meaning of the *seder* in her life:

> One of the things I like to do is a Passover *seder*. I make my own. The last few years, I've gotten together with a friend of mine who likes to do that sort of thing. So we 've co-hosted and that's great. I like leading the *seder*, it was what my grandfather did, and cooking for it is a huge part of my ritual for the holidays. I make my grandmother's recipe of gefilte fish from scratch. I've been doing that for a while now, and that ritual, in particular, I just love to do.

Through the yearly reenactment of the *seder* meal, this participant integrates the memory of both of her survivor grandparents (now deceased) into her ritual life. As a grandchild leading the *seder*, she replaces her grandfather as the culture bearer of religious practice; in the preparation of ritual foods, she assumes her grandmother's traditional role in the preservation of domestic rites. This narrative thus highlights the ways in which second-generation descendants transform ritualized gender norms to allow for the inclusion of traditions that are associated with their grandparents' cultural practices and that provide an emotional connection to the deceased.

Finally, the research on ritual and the intergenerational transmission of trauma also reveals the importance of cultural reclamation to a small but significant group of respondents whose survivor families struggled to maintain their Jewish heritage in a hostile postwar climate. This phenomenon was especially pronounced among survivors who, following liberation, returned to an eastern European homeland where the Jewish community had been destroyed and where Sovietization presented barriers and obstacles to the ongoing practice of Judaism. Unlike the Baby Boomer generation in the United States, the eastern European participants who were born into these post-Holocaust societies were affected by the absence rather than by the presence of ritualization in their family culture.

Religious Repression and Ritual Connectivity

Four of the respondents, three children and one grandchild, were born into cultures where the survival of Jewish tradition was threatened. Three case studies are cited here to illustrate the significance of ritual reclamation among these descendants and the strong emotional attachment to Jewish ritual that emerged from the experience of religious repression. The first case is that of a first-generation descendant who was raised in a Soviet bloc country until her family emigrated to the United States when she was fourteen. Here she describes the anti-Semitism she encountered as a child and her subsequent lifelong engagement in the preservation of Jewish tradition, although she herself is not an observant Jew:

> Spirituality is important to me but not as far as Jewish beliefs [go]; that is something different. What is important to me is Jewish heritage and the traditions. I love the culture. In [. . .], we experienced a lot of anti-Semitism in the schools and there was no place to go to be Jewish. When we came here, my father went to the synagogue every single Saturday, for years. For years, it meant so much. [My parents] were both in camps. They would celebrate Yom Kippur and I would celebrate with them. Now that they are not here, I go to pay my respects and because it is my heritage. I sometimes go on Rosh Hashanah and I always light candles on Chanukkah; I sing the song and I make potato *latkes*.

The second case, while also emerging from the social conditions of an eastern European postwar society, differs somewhat from the first in that this participant was raised in a Balkan country to which his family had fled when the Nazis occupied their neighboring homeland. Soon after they took refuge in the neighboring country, his mother was deported to a labor camp, where she survived the war, returning to the country of refuge in which the respondent was born and currently lives. The descendant, now in his sixties, has assumed the responsibility for maintaining a small prewar synagogue where a handful of descendants meet each week for Sabbath services. He also acts as a tour guide to visitors and, during a brief tour of the building, explained: "We don't do prayers. We never had a Jewish education or a Jewish upbringing. We come here [the synagogue] every Friday night to have a meal together. We light candles, we drink wine, and we bring in the Sabbath. We also use it for the [High] holy days, and sometimes tourists come too. It is important that I keep this. I don't know what will happen after I am gone." As one of the few remaining Jews in this eastern European city, the participant occupies a significant social role as the preserver of what little tradition survives and of the Jewish spaces that have been reclaimed by this descendant generation.

A third participant, a granddaughter of survivors, was also raised in a Balkan country. After marrying an American Jew, she emigrated to the United States as a young woman but returned to her country of origin to hold a traditional Jewish marriage ceremony, the first open ceremony in her town since World War II. For this respondent, the reclamation of her Jewish heritage and the religious culture of her grandparents was symbolized by an ancestral ritual act:

> I wanted to have a *chuppah* in [. . .]. We had the first public *chuppah* after sixty years in my town. The town where I grew up. There were some weddings before that under the Communists, but one way or another they hide or do it some way that [is] not officially recognized. We could be open and free, to do it publicly. We did it in the back yard of the Jewish community [center] with hundreds and hundreds of people attending. [They] came from all over and danced at our wedding. It was incredible. The important moment for me was such a bonding between me and my grandmother. I felt that symbolically I wore my white wedding dress for her because she never had a chance to when [she] got married before the transport, in the rush of it all when the Nazis came.

In comparison with the descendants who were raised with religious freedom, the eastern European descendants seek to retain traditional practices within an adaptive culture of reclamation that is signified by the historical repression of religious tradition, a phenomenon which illuminates the various social meanings that ritual brings to the lives of descendant generations, some of whom seek to innovate and change tradition, others of whom wish to re-create the rituals that had been suppressed by postwar Soviet society.

The findings in this chapter thus reaffirm the connective value of ritual and the role that religious rites and practices play within the emotional lives of post-Holocaust families. As the research suggests, ritual functions as a site of traumatic transfer, as a space of separation and differentiation, and as a link to a pre-genocide way of life that is invoked in the traditions of a threatened people and endangered religious culture. In turning to the sphere of religious beliefs, the research further highlights the importance of differentiation and innovation among succeeding generations who, while practicing and reinventing Jewish ritual, nevertheless question the traditional Jewish concept of God and divinity. Drawing a distinction between emotion-laden ritual observance and acceptance of religious doctrine, both those who were raised in the United States and those who were raised in eastern Europe have sought alternative spiritual worldviews in the aftermath of genocide. These findings are elaborated on more fully in the next chapter.

3

Redefining the Sacred

Spirituality and the Crisis of Masculinity among Children and Grandchildren of Survivors

The research on ritual, as elaborated in the previous chapter, highlights the ways in which children and grandchildren of survivors negotiate their responsibility for culture-bearing through the construction of new ritual forms and the reclamation of a suppressed religious culture. With regard to the spiritual worldviews among the descendants of the Holocaust, the findings reveal that, like ritual spaces, the realm of the sacred has become a site of transformation. As evidenced by the accounts of the participants, spirituality among children and grandchildren of survivors reflects a move away from institutionalized religion in favor of a more individualized approach to religious beliefs and spiritual orientation. This trend among descendants suggests that in the aftermath of genocide, succeeding generations seek a "break with the old order" (Berger 1967) through a reimagining of the divine outside the boundaries of patriarchal Judaism. In exploring the ways in which gendered notions of God are transformed by the social relations of ethnic/religious violence, this chapter considers the multiple meanings of "Godwrestling" within contemporary Jewish culture (Plaskow 1990). Beginning with a discussion of the religious culture in which the respondents were raised, the research explores the construction of a spiritual sense of self among descendants whose parents and grandparents often expressed a troubling and conflicting relationship with the biblical God of their Jewish ancestors.

Survivorship and the Intergenerational Transmission of Religious Beliefs

The research on religious beliefs among survivors of the Holocaust offers a wide variety of theological responses to the trauma of suffering and genocide. While the post-Holocaust debates among Jewish theologians and clergy tend to address the larger metaphysical questions of the existence and nature of God (Maybaum 1965; Jacobs 1993; Goldberg 1995; Cohn-Sherbok 1996), survivors of the Holocaust bring their own worldviews to the experience of survivorship that inform the meaning systems from which their children and grandchildren develop a spiritual sense of self. Previous studies suggest that while survivors of the Holocaust hold varied and often conflicting sets of beliefs, four responses to survival tend to be most prevalent: a continued and unchanged belief in the patriarchal God of biblical Judaism; a strengthened belief in God; a loss of belief in God; or a defiant belief that poses challenges to an abusive God (Marcus and Rosenberg 1988; Carmil and Breznitz, 1991; Blumenthal 1993; Waxman 2000). Further, the research reveals that within these varying religious responses, survivors express a broad range of emotions surrounding their feelings about God, including rage, a sense of abandonment, and gratitude for survival (Marcus and Rosenberg 1988).

As for to the narratives of descendants, respondents report that among their parents and grandparents, and especially their fathers and grandfathers, rage toward and fear of God were among the most predominant emotions that were conveyed in the post-Holocaust family. Typically, rage was expressed over questions of God's existence. In the following account, a daughter who was raised in a nonreligious home describes the anger with which her father addressed questions about God: "I would talk about God and my father would talk about science. I think science for him was like a religion. He doesn't really talk about God a lot and when he does it is in a mocking way that sometimes leads to anger in a way that he really relished. I mean you could just tell he was just like reveling in his anger when the topic of God came up." Respondents from more religiously traditional homes reported the confusion they experienced over a parent's or grandparent's rejection of God, even as he or she insisted upon strict adherence to religious law within the family. A participant in his early fifties explains: "It was weird mixed messages. [My father] was so nonreligious and pissed off at God and he couldn't believe any of it, yet he felt like he had to keep me in the *yeshiva* and be a member of the synagogue. And I always felt like, What are you talking about? You are saying this and you are forcing us to do that." This participant referred to his father's beliefs as a kind of "religious schizophrenia" in which God was simultaneously denied and feared. In this case, the responses of the survivor parent vacillated between a belief in the nonexistence of God and fear of God's punitive powers. As reported by the respondents, fear of God was particularly strong among those survivors who believed that in return for their survival, God demanded a strict adherence to religious law. A granddaughter of an Auschwitz survivor thus describes the culture of fear that permeated her religious upbringing: "My grandfather, who was one of the older people to survive, lived very close to us. And my mother was always afraid because he would go into a rage if we were not keeping all the laws and customs. So he would come over on Saturday and touch the TV to see if it was hot and if we had been watching television—he was a fanatic and his strong beliefs and fear of God overshadowed everything else, even his relationships with his siblings and his children."

The strict religiosity to which other survivors adhered was sometimes framed by the strong conviction that those who survived had done so because they had remained observant even under the harshest of conditions. Thus, strict adherence to tradition (described in the previous chapter) often emerged from gratitude and fear of God. A woman in her mid-fifties offered this perspective on her mother's religious observance and her belief that God had personally saved her from perishing in the camps:

> She believed in God and therefore she was spared. She thought that people in the camps weren't religious, weren't kosher, and that they might not

have believed as well as she did. She was stringent and rigid in terms of kosher. She had this personal relationship to God and that meant for example that she would often expound about God. She was very much convinced that her views were right and therefore God had recognized that in this personal relationship that she had with God he had spared her.

As these and other narratives illustrate, the religious undertones of traumatic transference created a cultural environment in which intense and sometimes conflicting feelings concerning God resulted in the creation of an emotionally charged spiritual terrain from which succeeding generations shaped their own understandings of God and/or the meaning of the divine. In response to their parents' and grandparents' fear, anger, and confusion concerning God, descendants developed a diversity of belief systems in which notions of the divine have been reimagined and reconceptualized. The varied spiritual worldviews that the descendants have embraced include both transcendent and immanent meaning systems that reflect a desire to create a more personalized and adaptive approach to an understanding of the sacred. As such, the nontraditional worldviews of the descendants generally follow two trends in modern religious thought in which spirituality is distinguished from religiosity in contemporary society. These trends are the belief in a personalized rather than institutionalized notion of a higher power and the search for meaning through immanence and personal forms of transcendence (Roof 1993; Spilka and Mcintosh 1996; Zinnbauer et al. 1997). In addition, the findings suggest that the spiritual legacy of the Holocaust can also be found in the rejection of the patriarchal God of biblical Judaism.

Belief in a Higher Power: Redefining the Masculinized God Figure

Within the social scientific study of religion, the concept of a higher power is associated with traditional forms of religiousness that highlight a belief in and relationship to an externalized and transcendent god figure or divine being (Zinnbauer et al. 1997). Within a Judeo-Christian worldview, the notion of a higher power is typically gendered and male-centered. It is thus significant to note that, although more than half of the respondents expressed belief in a higher power, their conceptualizations of the divine frequently challenged the patriarchal context through which the sacred is construed. In this regard, the participants tended to be cautious in their use of the term *God* precisely because of its gendered meaning, preferring terms like *higher power* that acknowledge the existence of a transcendent being without reinstating the problematic biblical God of survivor culture. A number of examples from the study will help to illuminate this point. In the first account, a woman whose mother survived Auschwitz refused to raise her children as Jews, creating in her daughter a deep spiritual longing:

> For me, I went through various phases in what I think about God. This is all stuff that I came up with. First, when I was a child, I decided there was no God. I asked my mother, "How come you didn't raise me Jewish?" I think she said, "How could a Jewish God do this to me?" That suggested to me there was no God. So I went around saying there was no God. Then I started thinking about the universe and how did things start and I couldn't come up with a scientific answer. So I thought maybe that is where the God piece comes in. God created the spark that started it all. That's what I thought for a long time, but it was never good enough. It wasn't enough. I walked around with this kind of emptiness. A lot of people have this void we are trying to fill. What I finally learned is that you have to fill it with a relationship to something bigger than yourself, a higher power. That is where I draw my comfort [from].

As this account reveals, the participant's belief in a higher power serves a number of important socio-emotional functions, the most significant of which appears to provide a personal connection to a divine being that offers comfort and satisfies a longing for spiritual meaning in the respondent's life. Another case, that of a son of survivors, offers a somewhat different perspective on the individual's relationship to a higher power:

> I consider myself an agnostic Jew. I have a very, very hard time believing in God [because of] what my family went through in the war. It kind of raises the question, If there is a God, why did this continue to happen, the persecution, all the way up to the killing, the mass killing? Where was God? But then my mother was only eleven years old, running and hiding. One of the many nights that they slept outside, my mother woke up in the morning and about a foot from her head was a big piece of shrapnel. I guess if there is a God, that is why it didn't hit her in the head and kill her. So I think probably there must be something, some higher power that looked out for her—her parents did not survive but she did. She escaped twice. How was that possible for such a young girl?

In this account, the respondent, rather than focus on his own particular needs for spiritual fulfillment, emphasizes instead the significance of the divine as a source of survival. Within this theological paradigm, belief in a higher power is tied a belief in a spiritual protector who is responsible for saving the lives of survivors, as another respondent explained:

> The strongest spiritual feelings I have actually center on my parents' survival of the Holocaust. Do I believe that it was a random thing? I don't. My mother didn't either. My mother was an incredibly spiritual person. My mother always said, "I didn't survive for me, and it wasn't for you. It was for the grandchildren, that is why I was chosen to live." I think there is some sort of a master plan. And I struggle all the time with the idea of something being predestined or not. Where does individual choice come in and where does the master plan, the higher power, change our destiny?

While this construction of a higher power as protectorate and savior is reminiscent of the qualities of a paternalistic deity, the gender of the divine remains either intentionally unstated or ambiguous in the language of the respondents, as one woman, forty-eight years old, makes clear:

> I have a very strong spiritual need. I pray a lot to a lot of different entities—sometimes to my ancestors or to the spirit of the holy mother. I don't even have a proper language for it. The term *god*—that's a male term and it doesn't sum it up for me. To try to put it in[to] words is hard. I have been thinking a lot about it lately. Who am I talking to? Who am I asking for help? The source of life? Whatever it is that made the world? I just know I believe there is a spiritual power out there that I can turn to for help and guidance.

Another respondent whose parents survived numerous death camps and raised their children within the Conservative tradition offered this insight into his relationship to the divine: "I believe there's a higher power. And part of it is, I want to believe. Because it is a crutch to help when things happen and you don't feel like you're alone. And of course I am not totally convinced. But I want to believe. I find comfort in that mindset and that with this higher power there is also an afterlife, some utopia where you don't have any worries and that it is a better place."

Finally, a granddaughter of survivors also expressed a belief in a higher power. Here she describes her spiritual evolution: "As I pulled away from the *mitzvot* [commandments] and the day-to-day interaction with the Jewish community, I simultaneously started searching for other interpretations of spiritual beliefs. What I found is a core belief—a higher power that has an influence in our daily lives. Nothing is coincidence. There's a purpose for every aspect of what you experience, day in and day out. And I do believe that."

As the narratives of higher power strongly suggest, children and grandchildren of Holocaust survivors have a deep-seated need to believe in a spiritual power that gives purpose to life. Because their worldviews have been shaped by the knowledge of their family's suffering, descendants express a belief in a spiritual presence or entity that offers the possibility of survival and thus the affirmation of the existence of a lifegiving force to which the descendants turn for comfort and solace. This spiritual response to traumatic transference, while challenging the omnipotent power of a patriarchal god, nonetheless preserves a belief in an externalized divinity through which hope for the future and for humankind is sustained.

Individuated Spirituality and the Turn toward Immanence

The turn toward immanence and personal constructions of transcendence constitute the second set of findings on spirituality among descendants. In contemporary Western thought, the concept of immanence has taken on a variety of forms and expressions with the development and proliferation of nontraditional religious movements, including those that are associated with Eastern religious ideologies and feminist spirituality (Christ 1979; Adler 1998). Within the broad spectrum that defines an immanent worldview, God or the divine is typically understood as emanating from within the individual, fostering a belief in an internalized rather than externalized notion of spiritual or creative power. Immanent belief systems are therefore based on notions of interconnectedness and faith in a unifying spiritual force. Among the participants in this study, close to half of the respondents adhered to an immanent worldview that emerged from their disenchantment with and rejection of traditional Judaism.

These findings are closely tied to Roof's (1993) study of new generations of spiritual seekers who, in rejecting organized religion and traditional definitions of God, turn to a more individualized understanding of the divine. While Roof's work focused primarily on the Baby Boomer generation—the age cohort of children of survivors—the research here suggests that spiritual seekership is also characteristic of the grandchildren of survivors, a post–Baby Boomer generation whose members, like their parents, have had access and exposure to alternative and non-Western spiritual traditions. Thus, the turn toward individualized immanence among succeeding generations of survivors is in part a reflection of the shifts in Western religious culture that have led to a greater knowledge of and interest in diverse spiritual practices and beliefs.

Of particular importance to this spiritual trend among descendants is the adoption of an immanent worldview that eliminates the boundaries between the self and the divine. The poet and Jewish theologian Marcia Falk refers to this unifying principle as the "indwelling" nature of the divine: "[T]he new *Sh'ma: The Declaration of Faith* states that the presence of divinity in the world is experienced as indwelling—that is, felt immanently—in all of creation.... The world we know—a world we may learn, through awareness, to love more deeply—is a multifaceted manifestation of a unified creation with a unified source; the many are One" (Falk 1996, 433).

With respect to post-Holocaust theology in particular, the writings of Richard Rubenstein resonate with Falk's perspective. A somewhat controversial theologian, Rubenstein in the 1960s proclaimed the death of God after Auschwitz. Many years later, having been influenced by Eastern teachings on spirituality, he reframed his belief in the divine through an immanent worldview: "In place of a biblical image of a transcendent creator God, an understanding of God which gives priority to the indwelling immanence of the Divine may be more credible in our era. Where God is thought of as a predominantly immanent cosmos, the cosmos in all of its temporal and spatial multiplicity is understood as the manifestation of the single unified and unifying, self-unfolding, self-realizing Divine Source, Ground, Spirit, or Absolute" (1992, 245–96). Rubenstein's turn toward a nonhierarchical unitive spirituality is evident in the accounts of first-generation descendants who, like Falk, incorporate diverse metaphors to describe the divine as a unifying principle. Among grandchildren of survivors, the path toward spiritual awareness reflects similar themes, as the following narrative suggests: "I try to avoid the concept of the old man in the sky kind of looking down and just observing. It's harder to define but I tend to visualize energy, you know, that is within as well as without—sort of like wavelengths and that can be anything surrounding us if we're attuned to them and aware of it."

Within the tradition of immanence, a number of respondents have looked to Jewish mysticism and Kabbalistic worldviews to evoke the divine within. Here a granddaughter of survivors, following her mother's spiritual path, turned to Kabbalistic teachings to find the in-dwelling nature of the divine:

> My grandparents came from very distinguished Orthodox families in Poland. My Grandfather's father was a *rebbe [rabbi]*. And he had devoted students who came from many miles away to study with him. . . . So my mother and I started this journey at the same time. It is gorgeous, very mystical. I have been studying the Kabbalah as much as I can. But it's still very surface level. The deep dark secrets of the Kabbalah don't really get revealed unless you are studying it full-time. But, every bit I've learned, I really love. I have really enjoyed learning about the *sephorit* [emanations of the divine] and how each have their own different aspect and energy surrounding them, how they interact with each other and how they are in each of us. That really speaks to me.

Menachem Rosensaft, the founder of the International Network of Children of Survivors, similarly draws on Kabbalistic teachings, reimagining the inner spirit as maternal and feminine:

> But what if God was not with the killers, with the forces that inflicted the Holocaust on humanity. . . . Think of the divine power, the spiritual strength of a mother comforting a child on the way to the gas chamber. If God was present at Auschwitz, it was in the mother, in her words, in her emotions, in the instinct that kept her from abandoning her child. . . . God permeated every Jew who held a dying parent, or a brother or sister, or a friend, or even a stranger. The mystical divine spark that charac-

terizes true Jewish faith, the *Shekina* [the feminine manifestation of the divine], was in every Jew who remained human to another fellow human being, and in every Jew who defied the forces of evil by risking his or her life to save a Jew. (2001, 190–91)

In Rosensaft's construction of the divine, he calls upon the maternalism of divinity, the power of life over death, and the source of human connectivity to affirm God's existence during the Holocaust. A similar theme is articulated in the narrative of a daughter of survivors who adopted the term "inner *bubbe*" to explain what she described as the "sacred feminine" within: "The inner *bubbe* is the inner grandmother who tends to people and makes sure they have food and passes on what people need to know and makes sure everybody's comfortable. It is this total nurturing inner goddess type. It's an archetype."

In comparison with a feminized construction of an inner life force, other respondents turned toward Eastern-based traditions to find a meaningful way with which to understand the divine and to experience the divine within themselves. The account of a child of survivors who was raised within Conservative Judaism illustrates this phenomenon:

> I practice yoga meditation. I've had some deep realizations and experiences. It's not easy, but it is very powerful. I feel a universal omnipresence that I am part of, and that God is part of me and I'm the little bubble in the ocean of God, ocean of love, ocean of supraconsciousness, so definitely when I go in[to] deep meditation that is my goal. Once you are in that deep ocean—that's what I call it because there is no body or mind awareness—it's just a split-second of one with the universe. It cannot be described.

Experiencing the divine as an altered state of unified consciousness is found in numerous other accounts, many of which reflect a longing to escape from the suffering of the human condition as it relates specifically to genocide. In the following narrative, a participant recalled, with great emotion, the moment she experienced her connection to the divine through the memories of terror that her mother had conveyed:

> I was in my early thirties. I must have been searching for something. I went into this community—there were other Jews there too, but I was an atheist. Then I started doing workshops and different forms of meditation. There was a teacher and they were teaching me how to do yoga exercises. I was chanting and trying to let go. I worked really hard at letting go of myself. One day, it all came together and what came up for me was the Holocaust experience. I was seeing dead bodies piled up. I was going through what my mother had gone through. That's when I knew I was directly connected to it. I was screaming. I was in a lot of pain going through it, but the pain was traveling through my body. I wasn't attached to it. At last I got out of my body. So I got to experience what it was like to feel pain but not suffer with it. . . . I looked around and I remember noticing that there was no separation between anything. It was all energy and it was all connected. That's when I knew that we were all connected. It was one of the gifts of my life that totally transformed my whole spiritual outlook.

The desire to transcend the torment of the Holocaust survivor is also evident in the account of a granddaughter who, raised as a secular Jew in Israel, turned toward Buddhism to find a way out of the consciousness of suffering:

> I became an official Buddhist last December. I've been studying Buddhism for five years now. As far as my beliefs on the world [go], the transpersonal realm, they're derived from Buddhism, not from Judaism. It's just a very different interpretation. It's not related to God, do this, don't do that; punishment and all that stuff doesn't exist. The notion of God from a Judeo-Christian perspective seems slightly childish to me, to be honest. I started doing yoga when I was nineteen. It's a

Hindu practice, but just a different consciousness, a way of exploring myself. Then I picked up my first Buddhism book, *The Tibetan Book of Living and Dying* by Sogyal Rinpoche. So many of the things he talked about, I just felt like I knew them. Like there's a concept called the Four Noble Truths. The first noble truth is that the world is suffering. Suffering is an inherent part of human existence. It's something that I've always felt, fairly young, growing up with my family. It was like everything I knew was in that book so I started to pursue my studies in the Buddhist community and then it all began to make sense. There is a notion of a creative life force, but it's something that is on a much larger scheme. On the most basic level, inherent in every one of us, is the potential of awakening and finding that place—beyond the self, beyond human suffering.

Through unification and connection to the realm beyond the materiality of life's pain, loss, and tragedy, children and grandchildren of survivors sustain a belief in the divine through a mystical path that is life affirming and through which the despair of traumatic transference is diminished. The belief in an immanent divine thus offers the descendants a way out of the consciousness of suffering that is the inheritance of their families' trauma.

The need and desire for a spiritual worldview among children and grandchildren of survivors, whether articulated as a belief in a higher power or the experience of divine immanence, highlight the importance of spirituality across a multigenerational culture wherein trauma and devastation are repeatedly remembered and where fears for the future persist. Thus, the research confirms that the descendants of historic tragedy and threatened annihilation, rather than turn away from religion altogether, seek to find alternative spiritual meaning systems to cope with and move on from the familial legacies of pain and suffering. Among this group of descendants, this trend in spiritual inventiveness has replaced an androcentric cosmology (Lord/God/King) with a nongendered spirituality, situating the rejection of patriarchal Judaism within the larger framework of the crisis of masculinity in which the Holocaust resides.

The Holocaust and the Crisis of Jewish Patriarchy

Starting with the work of Kaja Silverman in *Male Subjectivity at the Margins*, feminist scholars have interrogated the role of historical trauma in disrupting categories of masculinity in the face of male subjugation and violent warfare (Silverman 1992). With respect to the Holocaust in particular, this scholarship has taken a number of different turns. Among a significant group of scholars, the study of masculinity and the Holocaust has been associated largely with the rise and reinvention of Zionism within the Israeli national state (Boyarin and Boyarin 1997; Lentin 2000; Sered 2000). From this perspective, the politics of Zionism are framed through the humiliation of the Holocaust in which "its victims were presented as the quintessence and unavoidable outcome of the Diaspora and became essential to the creation of counter images of the *halutz* (pioneer and land laborer), the *sabra* (literally, the cactus; that is, Israeli born), and the Israeli soldier" (Zertal 2000, 102). In a further elaboration of this argument, Ronit Lentin, a daughter of survivors, suggests that, as Zionism emerged to restore and reify Jewish masculinity, both victims and survivors symbolized the passivity and weakness of the Jewish diaspora. Thus, the postwar Zionist patriarchal culture of the Israeli state created a counter-ideology and symbol system to replace the image of the passive and cowardly Jewish male victim (Lentin 2000).

Within survivor culture, however, the image of the coward and the weakling persisted. According to Susan Gubar, the dehumanization of Jewish men under the Nazi regime led to a "degendering and regendering" of Jewish masculinity among survivors, a response to historical trauma that challenged rather than reified male dominance and superiority. The failure of fathers to protect women and children destroyed the myth of male heroism while also exposing the fallacy of masculine strength and goodness. Postwar survivor culture, writes Gubar, thus became engaged in the reconstruction of gender "under the auspices of an eerie promise, namely the emergence of a post- or even antipatriarchal masculinity," a promise that developed out of a "cataclysmic break in the history of masculinity" brought on by the catastrophe of Jewish genocide (Gubar 2002, 252).

The crisis of masculinity that the Holocaust engendered is also the subject of Melissa Raphael's analysis of post-Holocaust theology. Drawing a parallel between the loss of the idealized man in the material world and the loss of the idealized heavenly father in the spiritual realm, Raphael argues that the post-Holocaust biblical God emerges as a weakened and emasculated symbol of divinity:

> In modernity, where divine claims, as much as any other, are subject to empirical verification or falsification in the eventualities of history, the dissonance between a God who promises protection and then, empirically, fails to deliver it will make theology ever more incredible. God can no longer be trusted. In other words, a modern critical theology looks to see if God could and did behave like a (meta) man. And if he did not it seems logical to some to reject God as having either unjustifiably withheld his power or as being merely ineffectual. (Raphael 2003, 35)

Within the narratives of descendants, it is the ineffectuality of the masculine God to which the accounts of the respondents speak. As the research shows, descendants of the Holocaust, in reimagining the divine in a post-Holocaust religious and spiritual framework, express disillusionment with the patriarchal God figure, turning instead to alternative images and belief systems that degender, regender, and demasculinize the meaning of godliness.

In comparing these findings with research on postwar Jewry more generally in the United States, one can make a number of significant observations. Since the 1980s, research on Jews and God imagery and belief suggest that Jews overall do not interpret the Bible literally or believe strongly in the notion of a judgmental God (Roof and Roof 1984).

Further, studies have found that God imagery among Jews, like like that among other denominations, remains largely paternalistic, though the notion of creator has replaced that of father and king as the more common representation. Among younger Jews and those of the postwar generation, God imagery tends to be more personalized and more open to an acceptance of maternal or feminine imagery (Roof 1999). Thus, when one compares the research on the descendants with studies on Jews more generally, the findings are consistent with a rejection of biblical literalism and a coinciding greater acceptance, particularly among younger generations, of nonmasculine conceptualizations of God that are in keeping with the cultural innovations of the late twentieth century.

At the same time, however, the meanings that the descendants bring to new constructions of the divine are deeply embedded in the traumatic legacies of survivor culture and therefore broaden an understanding of the process of spiritual creativity. Among the most well-known studies of postwar religion and spirituality are the well-referenced works of Roof and Robert Wuthnow (Wuthnow 1998; Roof 1999). Each of these scholars interprets the changing landscape of religious belief and practice through a lens of tragedy and disillusionment that marked the postwar culture in which the Baby Boomers (primarily white and middle class) came to adulthood. Referencing the cultural and political upheavals that affected the notion of God as a "personal, purposive being, perfect in goodness and supreme in power," Roof (1999, 74) identified the Holocaust as a catalyst for shifting notions of the divine:

> Contemporary religious pluralism and trends in science, rationality, and secularity have helped to shape, often out of a defensive posture, a generic theism. . . . In the modern era, however, growing numbers have come to find this generic view of God rather bland and uninspiring. With so much death and destruction, tragedy and evil in the world, some find it difficult to maintain a notion of an all-good, omnipotent deity. Although hardly the first to press the question, the boomers have grown up hearing about the Holocaust and have experienced much in their time. . . . (Roof 1999, 74)

To take Roof's observations one step further, the descendants of Holocaust survivors, whose knowledge of this cataclysmic tragedy is both personally and religiously informed, demonstrate perhaps a deeper need to challenge the "generic theism" of modern society. The interpretative frameworks that the descendants bring to the reconceptualization of spirituality reveal how those who have been directly affected by the destruction of the past transform traditional religious beliefs and ideologies.

In linking these observations to the feminist discourse on the demasculinization of God, an ideological shift that also has its roots in the Baby Boomer phenomenon, the findings reflect what Judith Plaskow refers to as "Godwrestling," the struggle to find spiritual meaning outside the norms of patriarchal religiosity (Plaskow 1990, 33). Originating within the field of feminist inquiry (Daly 1973; Gross 1979; Dufour 2000), the trend toward Godwrestling is also found among those individuals and groups whose lives have been affected by historical trauma. Similar to the Jewish feminist movement, the rethinking of God among Holocaust descendants has resulted in a diversity of alternative images and concepts that relate spiritual connectivity to nature, to the feminine aspects of the divine, to the unitary possibilities of religious experience, and to an active form of godliness. While the project of Jewish feminism is situated in the movement toward egalitarianism and inclusivity, for descendants of Holocaust survivors the turning away from a patriarchal god figure is more closely linked to the experience of disillusionment rather than that of inequality.

As the analysis of the narratives illuminates, rarely is the rejection of the biblical God framed within a feminist theological argument or the struggle for justice. What the findings suggest instead is that among those generations that inherit the historical traumas of the past, the break with the traditional male God is tied to the failure of the masculine ideal. Thus, it is not the injustices of the gender hierarchy within Jewish religious culture that has inspired a demasculinization of the divine. Rather, as this research has shown, the rejection of a masculinized divinity is in response to a genocidal history that has revealed the weaknesses and limitations of Jewish patriarchy. In rejecting the patriarchal God of their Jewish ancestors, descendants are forging new paths to spirituality that, alongside ritual innovation, give new meaning to the sacred within a post-Holocaust culture in which the legacy of trauma remains deeply embedded in the spiritual feelings and responses of succeeding generations.

4

The Social Relations of Inherited Trauma

The Meaning of Attachment and Connection in the Lives of Descendants

As the research on trauma and family dynamics illustrates, descendants of Holocaust survivors report a wide range of social and cultural response to the intergenerational transmission of trauma. In this chapter the analysis of the social dynamics of the postgenocide family is further explored through a discussion of the multiple ways in which attachments are formed, contested, and negotiated across generations. Expanding on prior research that documents the tensions and strains in post-Holocaust families (Bar-On et al. 1998; Gottschalk 2003; Wiseman, Metzl, and Barber 2006; Lev-Wiesel 2007; Stein 2014), the chapter investigates a diverse set of findings on relationality and connectivity among descendants. More specifically, the chapter examines attachment and strain across generations, the significance of extended family ties, death and connection in the realm of the supernatural, and the importance of place and belonging among descendants.

Attachment and Strain across Generations

Turning first to the children of survivors, first-generation descendants report a broad spectrum of feelings toward their survivor parents that reflect both their deep attachment to the survivor and the struggles of coping with a traumatized parent. The data therefore offer a fascinating window into the ways in which the trauma of the Holocaust shaped the bonds between parent and child in the postwar household. Within this relational sphere, children of survivors describe a wide range of maternal and paternal relationships in which love, empathy, anger, and confusion represent the complexity of feelings that emerged and reemerged within the emotional culture of family life (Wiseman, Metzl, and Barber 2006; Stein 2014). While the participants varied in their descriptions of their parents' emotional health, respondents frequently referred to their roles as caretakers of a fragile parent. In this regard, a number of accounts provide insight into the role reversals that typified the relationship between the child of survivors and a traumatized parent. In the first example, a daughter, the younger of two children, expressed the belief that she was born with the knowledge of her parents' suffering and thus came into the world with the responsibility to soften their pain:

> I think in general who they were and the pain I picked up from them was what affected me. Part of it is my belief system. . . . I didn't know if I was causing the pain, if it was my job to fix the pain. Whatever my unconscious experience was, my life was about their pain and how to make it better, whatever it was about.

The social responsibility to "fix" or care for a hurt or wounded parent was expressed by other first-generation descendants, primarily daughters, who as children somehow understood that their parents required a certain kind of attentiveness and care. Here the eldest of three sisters offers this perspective on the descendant child as caretaker for her mother:

> One of the things that [were] very hard growing up was that she would sometimes go into this place where she was like a very young child. We would have to mother her. It got to the point where I had very little patience with it. It was as if she [were] helpless. What I recall is that some-

thing would happen and her eyes would get really big and her breathing would get way high in her chest. She'd take these little quick breaths and there'd be this pervasive panic and anxiety. We would try and do nice things for her, make her tea, sit and hold her hand, wait through it. Poor mommy. It was like we were doing for her what she should have been doing for us. . . . There was this freezing up that would happen, needing to pay attention, sort of coddling her.

Similarly, another daughter, the eldest of three children, reported a role reversal in which "my mother told me things she should never have told me, personal things about her relationship with my dad. I became her mother and when my sister was born, I became the surrogate mother for my sister."

As research suggests, caretaking among children of survivors often results in anger and resentment for a parent who could not nurture and who often had little sympathy or patience for the problems or difficulties associated with a more typical childhood and adolescence. As one fifty-two-year-old woman recalled: "I was really angry back then. I was going through adolescent stuff—puberty, pimples, boys—and none of the stuff was important to her. It was like, I don't want to hear about your stupid little teen-age problems." Sentiments such as these were frequently expressed by participants who in adulthood gained a better understanding of what the survivor parent had endured and a greater sensitivity to their needs. One example of this shift in perspective is that of a fifty-two-year-old daughter who offered the following observation:

> [I]n retrospect, with some distance and more patience, I think I understand it so much better now, because when [my mother] was thirteen or fourteen, she was smuggling food into the Łódź ghetto. Then she was in a haystack and then she was in the city under this false name. And then she was in Auschwitz. So I have great compassion for her now, but as a teenager I was just angry. And to this day, I feel terrible guilt. It just pains

me. I was a little kid. What do you know? I wanted to be taken care of, to be loved.

In this life history narrative as well as elsewhere in the study, participants were reflective about their own emotional well-being. Looking "back" on themselves, they believed they too had been damaged or carried with them the social-psychological scars of having loved and been loved by parents whose lives had so recently been torn apart and who were struggling to parent while still coming to terms with their own loss and suffering. A son in his fifties explains: "When you go through second-generation stuff and have both parents [who had] been in the camps for long times, you have an entire lifetime of issues to sort out. And it's a lot of work. That's how I describe it. You marinate in a very very different atmosphere." Other participants also acknowledged what they believed to be their own forms of inherited trauma, as a respondent in his late forties described: "My mother suffered from depression and abandonment. She would go through periods where she would be obsessive about her past and it affected all of us, my sister, my older brother and me. It was tough. You live with all these terrible emotions around you and you can't help but feel some of that too. And you want to push it or her away. But then you feel so sorry for her." As this account suggests, traumatic inheritance is complicated by the descendant's conflicted feelings concerning attachment to a traumatized parent from whom emotional separation is also sought. The tension between longing for connection and the need for emotional distance from a traumatized parent was especially apparent in accounts that focused on conflicts that arose over social relationships outside the family, particularly with non-Jews, and the subsequent fears associated with the abandonment of Jewish religion and tradition.

Intergenerational Tension, Separation, and Negotiating Religious Conflict

The findings of the study strongly suggest that anger and emotional distancing frequently developed with social and dating relationships, especially with non-Jews. Because of the importance of Jewish identity and culture-bearing to survivors (Heller 1982), romantic partnerships with non-Jews, beginning in adolescence, became a significant emotional terrain on which intergenerational tensions were often played out. Here a respondent in her fifties recalls the painful period of her adolescence during which she began dating non-Jewish boys:

> [W]hen I was in high school and dating, and they were not Jewish boys, [my mother] would be waiting at home, sitting there crying, "I was worried, where were you? How could you do this to me?" And I'd walk in the door after having a nice time with my high school friends and I would think and say, "Basically, like, this is not about you, this is about me, you should stop playing the martyr." I couldn't take it. And my father was very much . . . the mediator between us because my mother would stop talking to me for days. You know there were lots of times of not talking and he would say, "The bigger person steps forward. You know your mother's been through a lot, the bigger person steps forward." I would say because of that, I know how to repair relationships. My mother and I are very close now and have been for thirty years, but the high school/college years were not pretty.

This life history narrative illustrates a number of significant aspects of the fraught emotional lives that first-generation descendants encountered as children of survivors who came of age as "American" teenagers. As with many participants, the difficulties associated with separation during adolescence were compounded by an emotionally charged family environment wherein separation from a parent also meant a distancing from the traumas of the past. Given the boundary confusion discussed in earlier chapters, this process of individuation was particularly challenging for first-generation descendants, many of whom, like the participant described above, developed attachments to non-Jewish romantic partners, often as a way to find connections outside the confining emotional sphere of Jewish family trauma. In this regard, a respondent gave this account of the conflicts she encountered with her father, a survivor whose first wife and children died in death camps:

> My father was more able to show attachment than my mother. He at least noticed once in a while when I did something right or wrong. He would go into rages when he got angry. I remember I was caught with a non-Jewish boy on the stairs and he chased him down the street and grounded me for a month. All I was doing was sitting on the stairs. For him, it was really wrong. It was directly the most important issue, picking someone Jewish. . . . I was trying hard to be a good girl, and I got to a point where I became the rebel, not being a bad kid, but doing what I thought was right. So at least I had some sense of self. But really that was my psychological struggle and it continued and continues today.

This respondent went on to explain how her eventual marriage to a non-Jew remained a source of deep tension with her father:

> We dated for four years before I got married, and during those four years my father refused to be in the same space. It was intense. Through that process, it was part of my separating process from my family. I invited all of my father's friends to the wedding and almost all of them decided to come, so it was a kind of letting go for him, letting go of control. So he decided to come and at that point he accepted it. But up until that point he was very angry and resistant.

Repeatedly, respondents highlighted how their choices to be with non-Jewish partners lay at the core of intergenerational conflict among survivor parents and how resolving these strains lay at the heart of their attachment to the survivor generation. This phenomenon was evident in both heterosexual and same-sex partnerships. In recounting the experience of coming out to her mother, a daughter revealed that her mother accepted her sexual orientation with greater ease than she accepted her partner's Christian background.

In almost every case wherein tensions and conflict were reported, the participants sought and achieved reconciliation over time, a trend that many of the participants attributed to the strength of the intergenerational bonds in post-Holocaust families. In one particularly striking case, a participant gave a powerful account of how the strains over religious tradition had filtered down to second-generation descendants. In this family dynamic, the conflict developed around the wedding ceremony of the respondent's daughter, a grandchild of survivors. The ceremony was scheduled to take place before sundown on a Saturday afternoon (the Jewish Sabbath).[1] In the months before the wedding, the grandmother of the bride, an elderly survivor of Auschwitz, expressed her disapproval and communicated to the respondent (her daughter) that she did not plan to attend her granddaughter's ceremony because the timing violated Jewish law. As the wedding drew nearer, the respondent as well as other family members asked the survivor to reconsider her decision, stressing the importance of her presence at this momentous occasion in her granddaughter's life.

The survivor, who was described by the respondent as strong-willed and thoughtful, considered the effect of her decision on the family and on her granddaughter. The result was that she not only attended the wedding but also fully participated in all of the events. Although these types of family strains are not unique to Holocaust culture, the respondent stressed the importance of the dialogue that she and others were able to have with her mother, emphasizing the difficulty of negotiating intergenerational conflicts that center on culture and tradition. In particular, the respondent sought to convey the ways in which survivors and their descendants are able to resolve tensions within the family, providing a model for change and reconciliation across generations. The respondent thus offered this assessment of the relational commitment that descendants and survivors have to one another: "I'm very proud of our family, that everybody worked so hard probably for three months and that we are able to repair and resolve and come to a place where my mother was excited about the wedding. I'm very proud of my mother, that for a ninety-year-old she was flexible enough to change and become part of my daughter's future."

It is important to note that in this case, the disruption to familial attachments arose over the second generation's breaking away from tradition, a finding that is confirmed by other grandchildren of survivors. One case study in particular illuminates the depth to which the anxieties and tensions over religiosity and social relations affect the socioemotional lives of grandchildren. In this case, the participant was a twenty-two-year-old grandson whose grandmother survived Auschwitz and Bergen-Belsen. In his lengthy account of growing up in a close-knit extended family, the participant explained that his mother was not permitted to marry anyone who was not Orthodox, much less anyone who was not Jewish. During the period in which the young man participated in the study, he was engaged in his own emotional struggles with his grandmother, to whom he felt very close. She had shared with him her stories of the Holocaust and he had accompanied her to Auschwitz when she was eighty years old. Because of his attachment to her, he was reluctant to talk to her about his religious doubts and to disclose the fact that his girlfriend came from a Conservative Jewish background:

> I just feel that [my grandmother has] gone through so much to be who she is. You know, my whole life I have felt like I am just hiding, I am not really an Orthodox Jew, I don't want to be. So you know it's hard for me to open up to her. I don't know if I should or shouldn't. I am just so scared, I just don't know. I just feel she is very, very, you know, Orthodox and I'm not so sure that I would rather have her [die] and me not ever [having told] her. Because I feel like when she passes she will be up there looking down at me and then she will finally see that this is my grandson, he

isn't very religious, instead of me like having to be straight up with her now. . . . I know she wouldn't be happy. I mean she would like want to be proud of her grandson. If I [were] religious, I could give her *nachis* [joy], but that is not the case. And I have a girlfriend [whom] I have been dating for many years and you know she ties into the story. She is Jewish. She grew up Conservative. At first I couldn't even introduce her to my parents, but then two years later I did and the family was understanding, sort of. But with my grandmother, we just pretend we don't know. I just don't know what to do now.

As a descendant grandson, this participant struggles with the dilemma of truth-telling, questioning whether he should hide the truth of his relationship from his grandmother while also shielding her from his own break with Orthodox Judaism. This account brings to light the deep and complex emotional attachments that second-generation descendants feel toward survivors. In the reproduction of Holocaust trauma across generations, grandchildren, like their parents, feel an obligation and devotion to survivors as they wrestle with the guilt and hurt that divergent life choices, especially with regard to Jewish tradition and marriage, create for a generation that has already suffered far too much. Like many of their parents, grandchildren feel a deep and continuous bond with the survivor generation. These ties are expressed in many ways—as love, as guilt, as compassion, and as admiration for their survivorship.

Perhaps the strongest indicator of this connectivity is the somewhat recent phenomenon in which descendants, especially grandchildren, are choosing to mark themselves with the tattooed numbers of their survivor grandparents. This trend has been reported widely in the news media and is also the subject of an Israeli documentary, *Numbered* (2012). The popular culture view of this phenomenon suggests that grandchildren are choosing to memorialize and honor the survivors through the reinscription of their death camp number onto the descendant's body (Stein 2014). In this study, one grandchild reported that he was considering this act of remembrance, although he had not yet done it. His rationale, however, was not framed in the language of honor and memory. Rather, he spoke of the tattoo as a bond that he could share with his aging grandparent, an embodied signifier that would "keep [him] close" to the survivor even after death. Thus, the reinscription of a grandparent's tattoo may have many meanings, including an act of remembrance and the strengthening of affective ties across generations.

Extended Family Members: The Social Relations of Kinship and Family in Postgenocide Culture

While relationships within the multigenerational family formed the core of relational ties for descendants, participants also cited the significance of bonds to extended family members who provided emotional support and continuity with the past. Within a culture of absence and extensive loss, the presence of other surviving relatives—aunts, uncles, or cousins—took on special meaning for descendants who looked to these relatives for connection, knowledge, and nurturance beyond the isolating world of the post-Holocaust nuclear family. As discussed in the chapter on narrative and identity (chapter 1), extended family members were often a source of information about the past. Here a daughter relates the significant role that her aunt (her father's surviving sister) played in her life:

> My aunt told me everything. She was twenty-one when she escaped. She was the youngest sister and was very innocent and she had red hair and blue eyes and she passed for Aryan. She was working for a doctor and the doctor said, "If you take this doll and deliver it to a hotel in New York, I will get you two visas. She just said, "Sure." So he gave her two visas. . . . My father was in jail. She want back to the town where he was in jail, she knew people there and she begged them to let him out. My aunt could always, she was a great woman, a very unusual person who could persuade people [of] things and she has twenty-one nieces and nephews and she was like the second mother to everyone. She never had any children of

her own. But she was like a mother, like my mother.... My aunt always wanted the cousins to know each other and love each other so she always would have a great big table and serve hot dogs and beans and things like that. She was great, she was great.

This account highlights a number of important functions that extended family members play and their social value to descendant populations. In this recollection, the participant's aunt acted as memory keeper, surrogate parent, and the tie that binds descendants to one another. Another respondent, a daughter in her fifties, similarly reflected on the critical role that her uncle played in her young adult life. Here she speaks of her father's brother as a surrogate parent with whom she felt a deep and close kinship:

My uncle was my second father. I first met him when I was sixteen. He was living in Europe. He was the one who kept me sane. This uncle liked to do everything I liked to do, to draw, to read. He was running a treatment center for kids.

As soon as I could, I went to work with him in the treatment center he ran. We wrote to each other all the time. There's a family piece, a little charm that was a tie tack that came from the Ottoman Empire. It is a star, and it had been passed on in his family from father to oldest son through generations and it hadn't been given to my father, it had been given to him. Instead of giving it to his sons, [my uncle] had it converted to a necklace and gave it to me.

Finally, a fifty-five-year-old male respondent describes his relationship to his cousin, a survivor of Auschwitz: "My cousin is a child survivor. She is a remarkable human being. She's really come out the other end of the tunnel. She's such a hero in my life. I look to her for advice. When I joined the Children of Survivors group, when I participated in events, what I tell my own children, it is my cousin whose opinion I really value." While these accounts offer examples of the significance of emotional ties to close family members, other, more distant relatives also provided a social safety net for first-generation descendants and their children. A forty-nine-year-old male participant reminisced about his young adult years when he visited his mother's surviving sister in Israel:

> I took a trip to Israel when I was in law school. One summer I went on a study abroad program and I ended up meeting all of my clan from that sister that had grown into grandchildren and so forth. That sister, who was the oldest of the bunch, had children who had children, and they took me in, open arms. I stayed primarily with her son who at that time was in his early thirties. They treated me—I mean I just had a wonderful time. That whole family was very warm to me. I met my mother's sister. She looked like my mother. It was, that was a feeling that was just wonderful because growing up here, I didn't have grandparents, I didn't really have uncles and aunts type of thing. When I first got there, they had a dinner party and I'm looking around saying, "I've got some relatives!"

Similar feelings were expressed by grandchildren for whom the existence of older relatives was especially valued: "When my [great-aunt] moved away—she was my grandfather's sister—we loved going to visit. She was so much fun. She was definitely a character, though, but she was fun. Yes, yes, she was fun to be around. Because we had such little family. That was it. There was such little family. So anybody we had was really important." Given the meaning of family ties among descendants, it is significant to point out that the longing for connection extended beyond the world of the living. In a particularly interesting finding of the research, a sizeable number of respondents reported experiences of the supernatural in which the deceased remained part of their relational life.

The Realm of the Uncanny: Attachment and Connection beyond Death

In her work on the legacy of the Holocaust among children of survivors, Eva Hoffman suggests that descendants "grow up with the uncanny... the sensation of something that is both very alien and deeply familiar" and that is not wholly based on "external realities" (2004, 66). Among the participants in this study, this sense of the uncanny was most often expressed through the experience of supernatural or otherworldly sensations that connected descendants to those who had died in the Holocaust or to deceased survivors with whom they had been close. This belief in the realm of the uncanny often framed their understanding of the intergenerational transmission of trauma, as one respondent maintained: "There's a collective consciousness and every child of a Holocaust survivor I talked to believes the same thing. Every person in our group said they agreed. We remember things and recognize people in our life we have never met. I don't know how that is possible."

Perhaps because Holocaust memory is so steeped in death and loss, descendants are drawn to a worldview that transcends the limitations of material existence. Accordingly, nearly a third of the participants made reference to a survivor's presence after death. Most frequently, the sensory awareness of the deceased was described in terms of a survivor parent's or grandparent's either watching over them or being present in their lives after death. A daughter whose father died thirteen years before offered this account of her sensory awareness of his ongoing existence in her life: "I went to a psychic once and she said there is someone that watches over you. I think now that it's my father. That's why I like to be in synagogue because then I know it's my father. I know he is there. I can really feel it." This case helps to illustrate the importance of place in the realm of the uncanny. This descendant's relational ties to her father were centered on the religious life she had shared with him before he died. The synagogue, as the primary social space of connectivity, therefore aroused feeling-states that invoked his presence. Another respondent, now in his fifties, also reported that his deceased parents were watching "from above" and were there for him even after death:

> I was very close to my mother, by the way, the most wonderful person in the world. And you know you imagine, you fantasize and sometimes it is more than that. Sometimes I say, you guys are looking down. You know what's going on. Hi, how are you? I hope things are great. I think about the kids getting bat mitzvahed and yeah, how they'll be there. You just kind of make yourself believe because there is comfort in it. They suffered so much on Earth, I see them in heaven with something so totally different.

Still for others, the presence of a deceased parent was felt in places where the survivor had lived before the war. This phenomenon is perhaps best illustrated by the narrative of a respondent whose survivor father committed suicide when she was a young girl. Having never totally recovered from this traumatic disruption to her life, the respondent, now in middle age, visited her father's prewar home:

> I was very close to him. My father was a lovely man, a very sweet man. When I was eleven and my brother was thirteen, it was going to be time for his bar mitzvah; my father committed suicide two weeks before the bar mitzvah.... A few years ago I made a trip back to find my father's house. When we were in this little town, which is where the house is, I found things that my aunt had always talked about. You know she told me about the wishing well—the well where they got their water and the barn and they had a lot of land and they had cattle and horses and they had hay wagons and all kinds of things.... I can tell you that for the last one hundred miles driving into this place, my father was in the car or on the car. I really felt that he was there and that it was, that we were together and it was wonderful, a wonderful thing. And everything that I had ever known about him, and I could see what he had lost. I could see that he

left places that were green and lush—it was so lush and overgrown. And he was there with me. And I could see the story of his escape.

For others, the sensory experience of seeing or feeling the presence of a deceased parent had more troubling overtones. One respondent recounted "visitations" from her deceased mother:

> When my mother died, we were living in California. A week after my mother passed away, my mother came to me, and I had a very bizarre experience. I had an experience where my mother came into the room and I felt a vibrational quality and I felt her trying to get closer to me and it was a very negative vibration. I remember it because my husband thought I was hallucinating after my mother's death, out of grief. And I remember saying, "Stop. Don't come closer." It felt bad. I don't know what it was. I could feel the vibration from her, just who she was. And she went away and I felt horrible. I just pushed my mother away. The next morning I get a call from my brother and he says, "You are not going to believe this. Mom visited me last night."

In recounting this experience, the participant expressed the guilt she felt in pushing her mother away, that even after death she sought a separation from her traumatized parent. In elaborating on this visitation and other premonitions that have guided her life, the respondent acknowledged that many people, including her husband, construed her extrasensory experience as fantasy or delusion. She, however, strongly believes that she possesses a "special gift" through which she has gained knowledge of the world beyond the living and that this gift is a legacy of her descendancy.

In one final example of this phenomenon, this same participant reported on her ability to see into the past, to become witness to the suffering of her parents and other family members, without ever having been given the facts or details of their survival:

My mother was from Poland. She wound up in a forced-labor camp and then there was something about Auschwitz and only her father survived. I had recurring dreams as a very small child, probably prior to age four, that I remember to this day because they were recurring dreams. The dream always started with a panoramic view of the city. And understand that at three or four, I had never seen cobblestone streets. I had never seen such structures. Every time I had the dream, I remembered that I had had it before, but when I woke up I didn't remember it. And in the dream there was a panoramic view of the city. It was like I had a camera and I was panning slowly. I could draw it for you, to this day. Eventually it makes its way to the train station. It's a wooden train station. There is nothing metal. The station house, I see some poles, the ties are wood. And I see a train track and after a few minutes I see a man running down the train track, screaming. I had that dream I can't tell you how many times. And one time I woke up afterward crying and my mother came into my room, and I remembered the dream and she said, "What's wrong?" And I told her the dream and my mother turned white as a sheet and she started to cry. She told me that she found out after the war, the Gestapo had come to take her family away while her father was out bartering food. When he came home, the family was gone. He heard they had been put on the transport and he ran down to the train tracks, crying, running after the train. She swore she [had] never told me that. Obviously I was too little. How would I know that at three years old unless—and I believe there is kind of a higher mentality.

While there are numerous and compelling psychological explanations for the descendants' belief in and engagement with the supernatural, what is of importance for the social transmission of trauma is the way in which the realm of the uncanny functions as a space of connection to those whose lives have been marked by suffering and pain. For the children and grandchildren of survivors, ties to deceased parents and grandparents are experienced through extrasensory perceptions that allow for an ongoing relationship in life after death. This finding illuminates the power of traumatic transference in shaping descendants' unconventional understanding and experience of the relational world.

Ancestral Ties, the Holocaust Outsider, and the Search for "Home" among Descendants

In moving from the realm of the uncanny to the realm of memory, my research now turns to the role of memory work in the social relations of descendants (Kidron 2003; Stein 2014). In her study of children of survivors, Arlene Stein discusses the importance of memory work, particularly among women who engage in genealogy projects and the search for ancestral homes: "A number of descendants remarked that they played the role of genealogist—tracking down lost relatives, constructing family trees, organizing excursions to their ancestral homes" (Stein 2014, 138). In keeping with Stein's observations, the findings of this study confirm the significance of memory work among descendants, although in the cases reported here both men and women embarked on explorations into the past. Through genealogical searches and journeys to prewar landscapes, participants sought to situate themselves within a larger kinship network and to create a sense of belonging to the prewar culture that survivors were forced to leave behind. Here a son who grew up in a refugee community describes his desire to construct a family genealogy and the difficulties he has faced in finding information on his father and his father's family:

> Both of my parents were the sole survivors of their families. They came to the United States through Boston. I did a lot of tracking, I have this family chart back to 1789 on my mother's side. She was from a town on the Czech-Hungarian border. I don't have any information on my father. In the last few years I have been trying to track down this information. I spoke to the group that brought him here. They say they have no records whatsoever. I said, "You brought millions of people to America. You don't have any record of them? No records for that period?" Right now some

>Polish friends of mine are trying to contact Polish offices to try to get documentation on my father's family. I got my father's birth certificate through a friend a few years ago. It took about a year. I have some new guys who are helping me look. Apparently this stuff is more available on the Internet now by the Polish government. The sites are in Polish of course so I need translation.

In a somewhat different but related quest for connections to lost and missing ancestors, children and grandchildren of survivors also seek out the rare photographs that survived the camps or that were among the few possessions of those who fled or went into hiding to escape deportation. As the sole visual memory of family members, these coveted photographs are considered precious artifacts that, within the research setting, were often proudly displayed by the participants, as if to say, "Here is proof that my family once existed, that there were aunts, uncles, grandparents, and cousins who lived real lives and who came before me." In this claim to a lost lineage, the name of each person in the photograph would frequently be recited, while the respondent shared what little was known about the deceased's livelihood, education, marriage, and/or place in the prewar community. "That was my uncle, he was a famous rabbi" and "My aunt was a musician and teacher" were typical identifiers that accompanied the narratives of the dead. The existence of photographs therefore helped to repair the familial break that lay at the core of the dislocation and disconnection of descendant generations.

As many of the respondents pointed out, a sense of dislocation and isolation defined their experiences as children of refugee survivors in a foreign culture. As part of the Holocaust diaspora, their families were outsiders within the dominant culture of the United States as well as within the larger Jewish community that had little or no understanding of what their families had suffered. Some participants thus spoke with bitterness about their outsider status within the Jewish community. A forty-eight-year-old woman who was raised in the Rocky Mountains region gave this account of her experience:

My parents were like outcasts. It's just, you know, it was just that they were not accepted into the American Jewish group. There were two kinds of Jews, the European survivors and the Americans. And I totally felt all through religious school that we were not accepted, that we were not natives many generations back. And I just remember my ex-mother-in-law, who was so religious and many generations back, and well known. I remember after seeing the movie *Schindler's List* and just crying my eyes out at the end, saying something to her, and she goes, "Yeah, it almost makes me cry." So to me, it just made me feel the American Jews were heartless, basically because they couldn't understand.

While other respondents were less critical of the Jewish community, many children and grandchildren of survivors nonetheless saw themselves as "different," both because of their ties to the Holocaust and the perception that their parents and grandparents had been held at a distance both by other Jews and in a country that had given them refuge. A descendant in his sixties poignantly explained:

I think I felt different my whole life. I've always felt different. It's one of the defining aspects of my character. For instance, I've never felt like a true American. I know it's harsh to say that, because I love this country and I feel very patriotic. But I read American history and I never feel connected to historical figures here. It may be because we weren't here. My people came here in the 1940s. But I think it goes deeper than that. It's more than just an intellectual thing. I've always felt a little bit like a foreigner in this country even though I was born here.

For a small but significant portion of these respondents, the sense of being an outsider led to a desire to return to the prewar home of their ancestors, a place of memory that held the possibility of belonging and that represented an imagined homeland of which they and the survivors had been deprived. Although, since the Holocaust, the notion of a Jewish homeland has most often been associated with the founding of the

State of Israel, descendants describe a more complicated relationship between survivors and their prewar home in which a sense of connection and even love was conveyed to their children and grandchildren. Like the trauma of victimization and loss, the yearning and nostalgia for a homeland was also expressed in the survivor's attachment to a prewar nation and place. According to the descendants, this attachment was passed on through identification with the survivor's European heritage and a longing for the physical landscapes of a European homeland. In the first instance, some respondents reported that their parents and grandparents never entirely lost pride in their prewar national identity. One respondent reported: "My father was always very proud of his German heritage. It was where he was educated and where he felt most culturally at home. I think that greatly affected me and even my children."

For other descendants, it was the invocation of the nature and beauty of the country of origin that was most strongly imprinted on their consciousness. In her study of Jews who escaped Nazi Germany, Judith Gerson and others (2007) discuss the importance of nature and the natural environment in the memory of immigrants. Similarly, the parents and grandparents of the respondents frequently invoked the physical landscapes of their lost homeland as the imagery through which fondness for and attachment to nation was preserved. The nostalgia for a prewar home was thus conveyed to members of descendant generations who turn to these ancestral landscapes in their search for belonging. This dimension of "inherited attachment" is perhaps most apparent among descendants who have chosen to reclaim the prewar citizenship of their survivor parents and grandparents. The trend toward reclamation, which is comparatively recent, has been documented in a 2012 article in the *Jewish Post and Opinion* that features a daughter and granddaughter of survivors who have become German citizens. In this account, the daughter offered these insights on her decision:

> Some survivors I know look at me like I am a traitor when they learn I have reclaimed my German citizenship. I cannot really answer these

questions as to why. Instead, I tell the story of Dad's obtaining his German license to practice medicine.... When people asked him why he would bother, Dad responded, "I worked hard for it and earned it; it was denied me. By rights, it's mine." Similarly, I was denied my German citizenship. It was taken from me before I could decide if I wanted it. I do want it. It's mine by rights. (Zimmerman 2012, 12–13)

In this example, the descendant draws on a "rights" discourse to explain her adoption of the prewar nation and home of her survivor father. Her decision, however, may also reflect a deeper need to "belong" and the desire to connect to the national heritage and culture of her father's family. In reclaiming citizenship, descendants are in effect "returning home." Accordingly, a grandson of survivors describes his efforts to reclaim citizenship in the Balkan country where his grandparents and great-grandparents were living when the Nazis came to power:

I think I experienced the Holocaust the strongest when I was trying to collect documentation about my grandfather so that I could get the living and work permit that I needed as a foreigner. I was going to the archives and having trouble finding these documents. The law on finding citizenship was written by nationalists and it was definitely not meant to help people like me. So the experience was very frustrating. My grandfather was the head of an import–export firm. When I went to the National Archives I met with the archivist, who was a very nice guy who had obviously dealt with a zillion people like me. He said, "Who are you looking for?" Because I was looking for something that said conclusively that he was of [...] nationality, I was telling him about the name and the business because we were thinking, where could these records be.... The guy repeated the name of my grandfather's business and said their sign was up on a wall that he passed every day on his way to school when he was growing up. That sign must have stayed up there until 1967 or 1968. He knew about the whole business and still it was difficult to prove my grandfather's citizenship. I think that is what really hit me and the frustration I felt. When I finally got citizenship, I had to tell the U.S. State Department that I had accepted citizenship of another country. I said, this was taken away from my family in 1939. You can't replace the people and I don't want money because I'd rather the money go to people who need it. But this citizenship is ours. Ultimately, the Holocaust was telling us we didn't belong, and you know what, we're back. So that's when I think I understood what it meant.

What is perhaps most compelling about this account is the descendant's wish to belong, to reclaim a formal tie to the country of his ancestors, even as that country had denied them protection and citizenship under Nazi rule. Hirsch thus concludes that "children of exiled survivors, although they have not themselves lived through the trauma of banishment and the destruction of home, remain always marginal or exiled" (1996, 662). Like survivors, descendants carry the experience of dislocation and a sense of alienation that compound the trauma of genocide. The quest for citizenship thus symbolizes a desire for home and nationality that is embedded in the memory of a pre-genocide European life and culture.

Through multiple forms of attachment and connection, this chapter has examined the social relations of survivor families that include deep bonds across generations and ties to ancestral cultures and nationalities. In the next chapter, many of these same themes are further explored through the participants' engagement with sites of terror—places of trauma and loss that invoke the past and in which descendant identity is reimagined and reconstructed.

5

Reengaging the Past

Identity, Mourning, and Empathy at Sites of Terror

Since the 1990s, descendants of Holocaust survivors have constituted an important and socially significant group of visitors to Holocaust memorials and monuments, including death camp sites, ruined cemeteries, and renowned deportation centers (Stein 2009b). In what has become a rite of passage, visits to these geographic landscapes immerse succeeding generations in the memory frames of Nazi persecution. As acts of remembrance, these trips are often undertaken collectively with parents, siblings, and other extended family members and frequently include multiple generations of survivors and descendants. In other instances, descendants have chosen to visit these memoryscapes on their own or as part of an educational program. In all of these circumstances, sites of terror provide compelling historical landmarks for the recollection of traumatic narratives that shape and inform descendant identity beyond the formative childhood years. In strengthening identification with the past, engagement with sites of terror facilitates the ongoing construction of a social self that is grounded both in trauma and personal as well as collective suffering (Zerubavel 2005; DeGloma 2009). To frame this dimension of descendant identity formation within memorial culture, the discussion begins with an overview of memorial sites as interactive spaces of social remembrance.

Memorial Sites and the Interactive Dynamics of Commemoration

Pierre Nora's (1989) groundbreaking work on history and memory provides an important starting point from which to consider how sites of memory function in contemporary society. Writing from a French historical perspective, Nora argues that museums, monuments, and places of preservation serve as archives of a past that might otherwise be forgotten. According to Nora, memory "takes root in the concrete, in spaces, gestures, images and objects" that "without commemorative vigilance" would soon be erased by the writing and rewriting of history (1989, 9, 12). While Nora maintains that the increased interest in and proliferation of sites of memory has led to what has perhaps become an obsession with archival objects and the materiality of remembrance, his work nonetheless suggests that it is often through these objects that difficult and contested histories are remembered and preserved.

Following Nora's observations, Robin Wagner-Pacifici and Barry Schwartz's (1991) research on the Vietnam Veterans Memorial in Washington, D.C., offers a sociological frame through which to consider how societies remember a difficult past. In investigating the means by which varied and sometimes opposing constituencies collectively create a monument to a troubling war, Wagner-Pacifici and Schwartz conclude that "whatever processes brought this cultural object into being in the first place, it is the use made of it that brings it into the life of the society" (1991, 416). Among its many uses, the Vietnam Veterans Memorial was found to function as an emotionally charged space for spectators, veterans, and the family and friends of the deceased. In this regard, the authors explain: "The names on the wall are touched, their letters traced by the moving finger. The names are caressed. The names are reproduced on a paper by pencil rubbing and taken home. And something is left from home itself—a material object bearing a special significance to the deceased or a written statement by the visitor or mourner." Thus, in their analysis, Wagner-Pacifici and Schwartz highlight the social dynamics that take place at the memorial, emphasizing the interactive processes that transform an "object of contemplation" into a place of connection, emotion, and remembrance. The insights that Wagner-Pacifici and Schwartz bring to the study of the Vietnam Veterans Memorial foreground more recent research (Fine and Beim 2007) on the interactive nature of collective memory and the way in which individuals construct meaning out of the past through interactions with memory objects such as those discussed by Nora.

Aaron Beim's (2007) work in particular highlights the interactive nature of collective memory, focusing on the way in which memory and meaning originate out of an individual's engagement with institutions of collective memory, including memorials and monuments. Through interaction at sites of memory, the cultural objects that these sites contain and represent form the basis for a "memory schemata" through which individuals cognitively organize, make meaning of, and interpret past events (Beim 2007, 21). With regard to Holocaust sites in particular, these spaces of national, group, and individual memory include a wide spectrum of memorial traces through which past events can be both interpreted and deeply felt. Intended to evoke strong emotional responses (Alexander 2004a; Alexander 2004b), these sites provide a social framework for interaction with atrocity artifacts as well as objects of memorial culture. With regard to the former, preserved death and concentration camps, for example, contain the buildings of incarceration and torture, atrocity photographs, remnants of the victims, and technologies of death (gas chambers and crematoria). Among the latter, the camps contain memorial books, gravestones, and shrines that commemorate death and loss.

Thus as sites of terror, camp memorials are illustrative of built environments in which the memories of a difficult past have been both preserved and restored through the use of material culture (Milligan 2007). As such, they provide important cultural tools (Wertsch 2002) through which memory is mediated and where "social actors bring multiple traumatic pasts into a heterogeneous and changing post–World War II present" (Rothberg 2009, 4). Accordingly, sites of terror are interactive frames of remembrance that fulfill a significant mnemonic function as described by Zerubavel (1996; 2005) in his work on social memory: "Consider, for example, the mnemonic role of ruins, old buildings, souvenirs, antiques and museums. . . . A visit to the National Museum of Anthropology in Mexico City clearly 'connects' present-day Mexicans with their Olmec, Mayan, Toltec, and Aztec ancestors" (1996, 292). Similarly, visits to camp memorials act as mnemonic triggers, evoking strong emotions among the spectators who become witness to a horrific past. In Jeffrey Olick's work on collective memory sites such as these thus constitute commemorative structures ("technologies of memory") that help to "shape what individuals remember" (1999, 225, 228) and that, according to Michael Rothberg (2009), represent the multidirectionality of memory spaces "in which groups do not simply articulate established positions but actually come into being" (Rothberg 2009, 5).

In the case of Holocaust descendants, the multidirectionality of these sites is evident in the framing and reframing of identity in response to a landscape that is evocative of the narratives and emotions that have been passed on by survivors. In their interactions with the artifacts and structures of traumatic memory, the descendants, like the visitors to the Vietnam Veterans Memorial, engage their senses—sight, touch, and smell—in a memorial landscape to which they feel deeply connected. In this respect, the camp memorials act as a transitional space of memory wherein the traumas of the past are communicated and further embedded in the emotional consciousness of succeeding generations, "providing a socially founded mechanism" by which the narratives of familial trauma are transmitted to Holocaust descendants (DeGloma 2009, 111). As the findings of this chapter will show, this process of memory transfer not only is found in the socials settings of death camp memorials but also takes place at cemetery ruins, massacre sites, and ancestral homes, places of familial terror that like the national monuments have become interactive social spaces where the children and grandchildren of survivors become immersed in the memory of Nazi persecution. More specifically, the findings illuminate the ways in which engagement with sites of terror fosters an increased internalization of anxiety and fear, a renewed connection to sorrow and loss, and the deepening of empathic bonds between survivors and descendant generations. In addition, the findings reveal several gender differences in these patterns of traumatic transference.

Reliving Atrocity Narratives: The Identification with Anxiety and Fear at Sites of Terror

From the outset, it is important to point out that in visiting sites of terror, either on their own or with surviving family members, the majority of first-generation descendants demonstrated a change in life course. Where previously they had made conscious choices to distance themselves from the trauma of their parents' lives, the decision to engage in the process of memorialization at sites of terror represented a shift toward greater rather than lesser emotional distance from their parents' traumatic past. In almost all cases this shift coincided with the aging or death of a survivor parent. As the findings of the study reveal, this turn toward the past facilitates the first generation's identification with Holocaust trauma in a number of important ways. Because these sites provide essential socio-geographic frames for the remembrance of suffering and loss, the immersion in terror landscapes results in an intensification of the descendant's identification with a range of survivor feeling-states, including fear and anxiety. This effect of traumatic identification was especially pronounced in those situations where a surviving family member acted as a memory guide, leading the participant through a landscape of terror in which a parent had survived. An example of this form of interactive remembrance is described by a participant who visited Auschwitz with a cousin who had survived the camp with the participant's mother. Here he recalls the day he and his cousin toured the camp together:

> We spent the day in Auschwitz. We didn't go on a guided tour. We didn't need to. My cousin was our guide. My cousin remembered a lot. This is

a long day. We're walking through all the monuments. We see the gas chamber, ovens, also the crematorium. She remembers the day they were liberated. My cousin and my mom and my three aunts were in a selection that day. My cousin was selected to go the gas chamber. My mom and her two sisters were not selected. My cousin's mom was also not selected but she volunteered to go with her daughter. They went through the door, down the stairs and were literally standing naked in front of the gas chamber doors when the *Sonderkommando* blew up the crematoria, literally at that moment when the Russians were about to enter the camp. They were let go. They were freed. And we went through the same doors and it was as if I could see my mother, standing at the door to the gas chambers with my aunt.

Although the participant had heard this story numerous times before, retracing his mother's passage from captivity to liberation while his cousin narrated the traumatic events lent a new perspective to the reality of his parent's trauma and especially to the feelings of anxiety and fear that his mother had expressed throughout her life.

In a further illustration of this phenomenon, a respondent in her late forties described the fear she experienced at Bergen-Belsen when she accompanied her mother to a commemorative event sponsored by the German government. In the following account, she reflects on the events that took place during the visit and her strong emotional responses:

It was the hardest thing I've ever done, without comparison. It was a surreal experience. The German government took all these survivors and carted us around in tour buses and did a sightseeing trip. We went to the train tracks where they were all brought in and where their stuff was taken from them. We went to the fields where the bunkers, the mass graves are and the cemeteries. It was suspended disbelief. It's like you want not to believe any of this is real, but you know that you have to believe it's real even though your self-protection mechanisms are saying, "This can't be real" . . . [The tour guides] had to feed 500 of us all at one time and they rarely had 500 chairs, which meant survivors and us [the children] were sitting on the floor in places that weren't being managed. Frequently, I was separated from my mother, whether intentional or not, but frequently we lost each other. Then I got the hint of what it's like to lose your mother in a crowd of strangers where they're speaking a hundred different languages and it's scary. I went through some of my own feelings that might have been similar to my mother's and I know how scary it was, really scary, to the point where you just have to go someplace else in your head or you can't survive. It is not possible.

In this account the interaction at the memorial site is complicated by the role of the perpetrator nation in bringing survivors to the camp to commemorate their liberation. Under these conditions of national memorialization, sharing of trauma narratives between survivors and their descendants is informed both by place and by the memory frames not only of the victims but also of the perpetrator/host culture.

As described above, first-generation descendants who accompany their parents on such journeys become both physically and emotionally situated in their parents' past, taking on the identity of a traumatized parent as they are led from site to site by guides who re-create, now as ceremonial rite, the experiences and feelings of the original trauma. Interactive engagements such as these "shrink the distance between past and present generations" (DeGloma 2009, 113), creating the social conditions under which traumatic experiences are socially shared and psychologically transmitted.

This effect of collective remembrance, whereby children of survivors have difficulty distinguishing between their own safety and the sense of danger that sites of terror invoke, is also found among the second generation. Although grandchildren tend to be less vulnerable than their parents to the social-psychological effects of traumatic transmission (Lev-Wiesel 2007), the findings of the research nonetheless suggest that like those of the first generation, second-generation descendants identify strongly with their grandparents' fears and suffering. In this regard, the findings confirm the role that grandchildren often play as generational links for the transfer of Holocaust memories (Fossion et al. 2003). This phenomenon, as discussed in chapters 2 and 4, is particularly apparent in those families in which grandchildren developed close emotional ties to survivors. Among these participants, visiting sites of Holocaust terror evoked similar responses of identification and extreme anxiety that were found among those of the first generation. Although many grandchildren of survivors believed that they already knew about the horrors of the Holocaust from family stories, such knowledge did not prepare them for the lived experience of previously imagined terror. This was particularly true for those participants who visited camp sites with a survivor grandparent. Here a twenty-two-year-old grandson describes how it felt to be at Auschwitz and Bergen-Belsen with his grandmother, a survivor who had planned this trip specifically for the edification of her descendants:

> She was walking me through the camp and I remember being in the camps, walking around the camp with her, where all the bunkers were lined up and she was able to point, like, "That was mine." She said, "We really had it bad." It was there I learned most of what I know. How her hair changed color, how she worked in the munitions factory and how her sister died from typhus right there in front of her at liberation. It was terrible. I could see it in her eyes and I started to feel like what it must have been like for her. She was seventeen and I am not that much older and here I was, seeing myself in these places.

In another case, a twenty-seven-year-old granddaughter organized a tour to Treblinka that included her parents and her survivor grandmother:

> We went to Treblinka. The first night we went to Treblinka, the city. We went to the hotel. When we went out in the morning, we were in the car, my grandmother did not look out the window, she was reading a book.

Then we came to the camp. I remember, you are there and you feel the dead people around you. You just do. You can smell it. . . . You go in the forest and then you come to the stone with the sign and you go in. The minute you go in and you see the memorial, I saw them, the three of them together, my grandmother, my dad, and my mom. We found the stone from my grandmother's village. We had candles. My Dad was crying and I was crying. It was very hard. Being there with my grandmother was really hard. It was not like before. I could see her pain and feel her fear. I just wanted to leave. [My grandmother] said, "No more, it's enough for me. Let's go." I felt the same way. I just wanted to get out, to leave.

By comparison, other second-generation descendants reported visiting death camps as part of high school educational trips rather than with family members. These accounts too reveal the impacts of these sites on their identification with survivor fear and anxiety. A respondent who was raised in eastern Europe explained:

I remember that I heard stories before from my family members and I read books that were in my grandparents' library. I read a lot of literature about Jewish destiny during the war and about the Holocaust itself. I read stories from people who survived Auschwitz and I saw the drawings. But it didn't matter. The moment I was there it just didn't matter. It shocked me so much. It was the feeling. It was stronger than anything I expected. I think it still resonates with me. I think of my grandmother and how her sister died and I realize now what freedom is. I could walk in both directions—in and out—but my grandmother's sister could only walk in. And it just hit me afterwards, when I was sitting on the bus on the way home, that we are just going back home, passing the gate, just leaving. Until then I don't think I really knew what it felt like to be so scared and trapped. When I got home, I got sick. I remember I got really sick when I got back, physically sick. It just transformed into sickness. My mom knew right away. She knew right away what was going on. I didn't try to hide it.

Similarly, another grandchild, now twenty-eight, gave this account of a high school trip to Holocaust sites in Poland:

> I remember vividly that we had a connecting flight in Frankfurt. The German soldiers, the way they dressed is very much like how the Nazi soldiers were dressed, just without swastikas. I saw that and I was like, I can't do this. I stopped and turned around. I kept thinking about my family, the ones who lived and the ones who didn't. I was very scared. I didn't like being in Germany. I wanted to get out as soon as I could. I was really scared of just being in the airport. Then we went to Poland and it was like seven days, seven days which was cemetery, ruined synagogue, death camp, death camp. Your days are full with Treblinka, Auschwitz, Majdanek, Sobibor. You stand in gas chambers. You're standing here, your family stood here, and there are Zyklon B cans and you're numb but also terrified. I kept imagining it was me and that I was my grandmother and somehow we got out. There was something so emotional. When I got home, I couldn't go to school for days. There was a ceremony and I read a paper about my family but as soon as it was over, I ran out the door and I was shaking and crying.

As the foregoing accounts illustrate, visits to death and labor camps illuminates the importance of place as a catalyst for the transfer of traumatic memory. While the presence of the survivor generation intensifies the identification with fear and anxiety, even in the absence of survivors, the trauma landscape is itself a powerful trigger for traumatic associations that remain embedded in the descendant's consciousness.

Further, as the diversity of narratives reveals, the identification with survivor trauma also emerges at other Holocaust-related places, including prewar residences and villages that function as sites of terror and violence within the collective memory of the respondent's family. In one such case, a participant returned to her family's prewar home, a small German town where her mother and father had lived. In the postwar narratives of family remembrance, this area of Germany was recalled both as an idyllic village as well as a place of terror where neighbors had become enemies overnight. As this respondent, fifty-two years old, described her visit to this small German town, her account reflects the extent to which she identified with her parents' anxiety and fear:

> I went to visit some family we still had there. It was scary. If a dog [barked], I would jump. I twitched. I was hyper-vigilant the entire time I was there. People were very kind to us, these friends and family. It was a sort of wondrous trip, in part some really strikingly awful moments. I apparently looked like Mother did when she lived there. I literally walked into town and people's heads turned and they called my mother's name, as if my mother had come back. The number of people who recognized me immediately was mind-boggling. It wasn't my favorite thing to go back as my mother. The scariest, creepiest thing was I knew who had done what, which neighbor had done what to whom. My father's business was taken over by a Nazi. I was standing outside looking at the house and I could see someone inside looking at me through the curtains. He came downstairs. He was about my parents' age. He stuck out his hand to shake my hand in the German way, and my hand developed atrophy at my side. It wouldn't move. There was nothing I could do to get into the social grace, now take your hand out and shake his hand. I was having a hysterical reaction, I guess, my hand was not moving anymore.

This narrative reveals a number of important aspects of the descendant's identification with the traumas of her survivor parents. The fear she feels in Germany is palpable, despite the kindness she was shown on her trip. In her visit to the town, the identification with her parents' traumatic history is powerfully acted out, first in the respondent's response to having been mistaken for her mother and second in the paralyzing fear she experiences at her father's former home. This account thus illustrates the ways in which the child replaces the parent in a landscape of traumatic memory, arousing deep anxieties and fears in the succeeding generation.

A number of psychological studies of children of survivors have found similar forms of identity confusion (Kellerman 2001c), suggesting that the merging of identity between the child and a survivor parent may have a gender component as well (Davidson 1980; Vogel 1994). Miriam Vogel's study of psychic trauma among children of Holocaust survivors concluded that, because of gender socialization and the relational dynamic of girls' development, daughters are more likely to have a stronger identification with a traumatized parent than sons. Consistent with Vogel's findings, identification with anxiety and fear was found to be more prevalent among women respondents who more frequently reported that they experienced themselves as victims of Nazi terror in the traumatic settings of Holocaust memorial culture. I now turn to the second set of findings, those that examine the identification with sorrow and grief, and a somewhat different gender pattern emerges. In contrast to reports of anxiety and fear, accounts of grief and sorrow at sites of terror were more commonly, though not exclusively, reported by men in the study.

The Identification with Sorrow and Loss: Acts of Mourning at Sites of Terror

Although it is difficult to disentangle narratives of atrocity from narratives of loss, the research on engagement with sites of terror indicates that these interactive forms of memorialization involve a complex set of emotional responses that include sorrow and despair, as well as anxiety and fear. While in some cases participants report a vacillation between sadness and anxiety, more typically there is a clear distinction between those respondents who carried the sorrow of their parents and those who were more informed by fear. With regard to the former, sons were more likely to provide accounts in which sites of terror were treated as gravesites where rituals of mourning were enacted, evoking feelings of loss and deep sadness. As with the research on anxiety, this finding may be an outcome of differences in gender socialization whereby the men in the study were more comfortable sharing narratives of grief rather than accounts of fear. In the following account, a fifty-five-year-old descendant recalled accompanying his father to the cemetery where his father's adolescent sister had been buried in the aftermath of a violent ghetto assault. In this narrative he remembers in great detail the search for family graves and his connection to his father's loss:

> We spent two hours in the Jewish cemetery. The cemetery was gorgeous. You could see how beautiful a place it had been. But it was destroyed. Stones were broken in half. All the marble was taken or stolen. It was a very sad, sad place to be. It was overgrown, literally, like a jungle. We found my grandfather's stone, the person I was named after. We found my dad's mother's stone. Then the most intense moment was when we found my father's sister's stone. He buried her there in 1941. She had something happen in the ghetto where a couple of SS got her. I don't know if they raped her or what went on. She went into shock from the experience. She was diabetic. My dad got her outside the ghetto and got her to a hospital. He was in the hospital with her when she died. He took her and dressed her up as if she were alive and carried her on to this wagon, a rented wagon. From the ghetto gates, he had to carry her to his home inside the ghetto so they could do the ritual washing of the body. So they did that and he buried her with a little headstone. He was obsessively determined to find the stone. And I found it. I found this stone. He was very close to her. Of all the people in the family, he was closest to her.

Later in the trip, this respondent visited Treblinka, where most of the other family members had died:

> When we got to Treblinka it was very strange. You drive up and you've got this building there, kind of an entry building there.... We took off and started to wander through the grounds. You walk in and there's a wooded section and replicas of train tracks and stone monuments that have stories in English, Hebrew, Yiddish, and Polish. Then you come into

the big field and there's a huge monument with all broken headstones for the towns all around, surrounding, with the big tar pit. We looked and found the headstone for our town. That was a very intense, sad moment. There was a guest book. . . . My dad wanted me to write for him in the book. I started to write in the book and the names started pouring out, all of these names of people that I had never known. That was the time I realized that this is where it was, Treblinka was the place where the whole family was wiped out. It was so intense. All the sadness they felt was also in me. It's in me, no question. I picked up my dad's intense feelings around this, and memory of most of it.

In this account, the memorial at Treblinka provides an emotionally powerful setting for the transmission of grief from father to son. Through the collective ritual of mourning and the writing of the names of the dead, the respondent felt the extent of his father's tragedy and suffering as well as his own connection to a family that had been exterminated before he was born. Within this interactional framework, memorialization both at the cemetery and at the death camp ruins linked the descendant not only to a parent's sorrow but also to his own feelings of familial loss.

The importance of sorrow and loss for the intergenerational transmission of trauma is further illuminated in the narrative of a twenty-year-old grandchild of survivors whose great-uncle died at Majdanek. A year before the respondent visited the camp, his grandfather received a letter notifying the family, nearly sixty years after the fact, that his brother had died in the gas chambers:

I made a copy of the letter that the Red Cross had sent and I had my *zaidy* [grandfather] write something in Yiddish to make a final message to his brother because I was going to bury that letter in the crematorium at Majdanek. Interestingly, I found out later that what he wrote was that he missed him so much and wished he could have seen him one more time. He also wrote that hopefully one day the Germans would get what they deserve for what they did to us. He wrote what you wouldn't have expected him to write. I remember the exact date I went. It was July 3. Majdanek's in Lublin. Everything is still intact. There are factory buildings all the way around. I remember we finally reached the crematorium. There's a bar that separates you from the crematorium. I read the whole letter out loud, said a few thoughts as if my great-uncle were with me. I said a prayer and jumped over the bar and buried it deep within the oven. I made sure that I put it at the very far end so that nobody could get it. I don't know if anybody did but that's how I left it. It was my way of saying that I never met you and I wish I [had] known you. Wherever you are I love you even though I never knew you. It was my way of saying goodbye to my great-uncle for my *zaidy*.

Like the accounts of the first-generation descendant at Treblinka, this narrative reveals the function that sites of terror serve in linking succeeding generations to feelings of loss for family members whose deaths are felt more intensely at places where the violence occurred. For this young respondent, reading his grandfather's letter at Majdanek not only fulfilled a responsibility to his grandfather but also established his own affective tie to his grandfather's brother. Rites of mourning at sites of terror thus help to create closure for survivors and a means by which succeeding generations emotionally connect to family members whose memory has been filtered through the trauma of their families' loss. Here as elsewhere in the respondents' accounts, Holocaust sites serve as places of memorialization as well as spaces of memory transfer where the events of the past are recalled through the exchange of emotions during the recollection of traumatic family histories. In the foregoing examples, children and grandchildren of survivors act as memory keepers for the families, seeking out objects of memorialization that connect both the survivor and the descendant to a traumatic past. The exchange of emotions that accompany these engagements with sites of terror intensifies the connective bond between generations, strengthening the empathic attachment between survivors and their descendants.

Acts of Remembrance and Empathic Bonding at Sites of Terror

Thus far in the analysis, the role of memory in the formation of survivor identity at sites of terror has focused on the engagement with the emotional dimensions of traumatic memory as these are expressed through feeling-states associated with fear, anxiety, sorrow, and loss. While gender appears to inform these two sets of findings, the data on the strengthening of empathic ties between children and their survivor parents reveal fewer gender differences in empathic identification. Further, given the often complicated relationships between first-generation descendants and their parents, the findings on empathic bonding at Holocaust memorials relate more strongly to children rather than to grandchildren of survivors. Previous research on empathic attachment in post-Holocaust families points out that, especially during adolescence and young adulthood, children of survivors tend to develop conflicting feelings toward their traumatized parents (Gottschalk 2003; Stein 2009b). In his work on emotion management among children of survivors, Gottschalk discusses the child's need to suppress anger and guilt-laden "negative emotions." Accordingly, as elaborated in the previous chapter, a number of respondents report an emotional legacy of unresolved anger that, because of their parents' suffering, could never be expressed. Descendants thus describe a form of compromised empathy in which the child, deeply aware of a parent's suffering, nonetheless develops a conflicting set of emotional feelings that includes anger, guilt, and what Stein describes as "cold detachment" (2009b, 42).

Given the emotional tensions surrounding empathic connection, sites of terror provide an emotional setting for repairing and forging empathic bonds across generations and thus serve as spaces of both traumatic identification and empathic connectivity. In this regard, one respondent explained that when she went to Auschwitz with her father, the site where his mother had perished, it was the first time she had ever seen him cry. Witnessing the expression of emotion in her elderly parent, she felt not for the first time but in a decidedly different way the suffering of the child/father who survived the horrors of genocide as a young orphan. Her empathy for him was thus both renewed and strengthened during their visit to the death camp.

For a number of other participants, returning with elderly parents to the places of traumatic suffering led to the retrieval of new memories on the part of the survivor and consequently a new appreciation for the extent of parental suffering on the part of the descendant. This phenomenon is illustrated in the account of a middle-aged daughter who traveled to Auschwitz and Bergen-Belsen with her mother, offering this recollection:

> One night, while on the trip, she woke up in the middle of the night crying. I knew that was bad. I talked to her about it. She started remembering things, stealing a loaf of bread from the kitchen because a woman she was friends with was very, very sick, like dying sick, and needed more nutrition or she wasn't going to make it. She was a Ukrainian. Apparently there were different camps for different nationalities. I don't know if these were Jews. But they attacked her, they physically attacked her and I know that traumatized her. They took the bread. Stories like that came back to her that she never told me. Going with her, hearing these stories, I could understand my mother's experience more, I could empathize more but I know now it is only a small percentage of understanding of what they really went through, how they could survive.

As this account reveals, the interactive nature of traumatic remembrance at sites of terror can result in the triggering of new memories for survivor parents. In recalling experiences in or near Nazi landscapes, parents and children thus engage in the sharing of new narratives and emotions that in turn lead to greater empathy among first-generation descendants whose own emotional states have been altered by their immersion in the memorial structures of Nazi genocide.

Further, the very nature of such a journey, when undertaken as a parent–child act of collective remembrance, extends the interactive aspect of traumatic immersion beyond the sites of memory. In a number of cases, such as the one cited above, respondents shared living spaces with a survivor parent. These trips thus provided an encapsulated social world for the sharing of memories and feelings both during the interactive phase of commemoration at the sites and in privatized social spaces where respondents returned, at the end of the day, to process their immersion experiences. A fifty-four-year-old male participant described how each night, after visiting the places where his father and mother had suffered and where his extended family died, he and his father would talk long into the night about the painful and horrific aspects of survival:

> We talked a lot. During that whole time I was with my dad. We shared a room the whole time. In Germany, Poland, and the Czech Republic. It did for our relationship what nothing else could have done. We had this bonding between us. We spent so much time together just talking and sharing. That trip was the most important single event that I've ever done in my life. It was a transforming situation. The fruits of the trip are still born now, more than ten years later—the feeling of how important it is to leave a legacy, to not forget, and to leave some mark and some sort of understanding. I at least now have my own understanding of what happened. What's there to be gained and learned from me growing up as a second-generation [child of survivors]. It's huge. I'm fairly settled inside myself and fairly clear now about the meaning of it. But no one who goes through this is ever done with it. My father died two years ago and I am so thankful that we were able to do this trip together.

In this way, creating collective memories at sites of terror fostered the growth of intimacy between parent and child. In engaging both with the structures of traumatic memory and the feeling-states that such structures elicit, the descendants of the Holocaust gain a deeper connection to their parents' suffering, even as they may feel overwhelmed by the incomprehensibility of the catastrophe of their parents' lives.

It is significant to note that both daughters and sons reported this shift in empathic attachment to their parents. This finding suggests that while daughters are frequently characterized as more empathic than sons (Surrey 1991), under conditions of traumatic remembrance gender differences in empathic bonding become less important. Because visits to sites of terror reduce the emotional distance between the children of survivors and their parents, first-generation descendants move closer to a shared victimized identity with survivors. At the same time, the interactive nature of this type of terror-based memorialization also reminds the children of survivors that their identification with parental suffering, while intensely emotional, is not the same as having lived through the original trauma, as the following account makes clear: "Once you have been to the camps, once you have had the experience of trauma, it's like I can understand my mother's experience more but we can never give to ourselves a percentage of what they really went through. How can you understand? You can empathize, but can't ever totally understand. Just being there you at least get a sense of what it must have been like, what she must have felt—how scared she must have been."

While the interactive qualities of remembrance at sites of terror may intensify the knowledge of and emotional connection to the past, the engagement with the material culture of traumatic histories can also lead to a greater awareness of the differences between the "inheritance" of trauma and the firsthand experience of genocidal suffering. Thus, the social realism of these sites can help to remedy the problematic consequences of "postmemory," as described by Hirsch (2008, 106), in which the survivor's trauma displaces the descendant's own experiences and memories. As the narratives, especially of empathic growth, reveal, immersion at sites of terror brings into sharper relief the emotional and experiential divide between the lived experiences of the descendants and the traumatic victimization of their survivor parents. Accordingly, they provide an interactive social network through which both the stories of the survivors as well as the stories of their descendants are brought into greater rather than lesser focus, diminishing the effects of postmemory on succeeding generations.

Overall, the findings in this chapter reveal how narratives of family remembrance are given new meaning in spaces of memorial culture, reaffirming that sites of memory serve as interactional webs where meanings are constructed by the families of survivors (Wagner-Pacifici and Schwartz 1991). Through interaction with the landscapes and material objects of Nazi genocide, the descendants of the Holocaust connect to the anxiety, fear, loss, and sorrow of their families. This connective dynamic of memorialization results in the development of stronger empathic ties to the survivor generation, contributing to a social identity that is marked by the memory of victimization. In bringing the trauma of the past into the present, these sites arouse strong feelings and emotions that connect descendants both to a sense of place and to familial suffering, as they experience through their own visual and emotional lens the places of tragedy that represent despair and survivorship. Immersion at sites of terror thus strengthens an identification with familial and historical catastrophe, deepening the descendant's role as carrier of the memories and traumas of the Holocaust.

6

Descendants as Holocaust Carriers

Bringing the Past into Public Consciousness

Throughout the previous chapters, the study of the intergenerational transmission of trauma has focused on the ways in which descendants become trauma carriers through identification with and attachment to survivors and survivor culture. This aspect of traumatic inheritance reveals the descendant's responses to a parent's or grandparent's suffering and the internalization of the trauma and pain of the past. For a portion of descendants, this aspect of trauma-carrying crosses over into the public realm. In film, memoir, art, and commemoration, descendants have emerged as a publicly identified carrier group for the telling and retelling of the Holocaust story. Drawing on Weber's concept of cultural carriers and threatened populations (1968), this chapter considers the social mechanisms whereby descendant populations have become "agents" for the reproduction of trauma for the larger society (Alexander 2004a), thus solidifying their social role in the creation of cultural memory (Bartmanski and Eyerman 2011). Within this analysis, the research explores the multiplicity of representations that have come to characterize Holocaust-carrying in public and cultural institutions, including the telling of survivor stories by descendants and the production of descendant narratives and art. The discussion of Holocaust carriers and public discourse will begin with an investigation into the role of Holocaust descendants in public acts of remembrance.

Holocaust Remembrance Day and Multigenerational Carriers

Holocaust Remembrance Day, *Yom Hashoah Vehagvurah* (Day of Holocaust and Heroism), was established in Israel in the 1950s as a day "dedicated every year to remembrance of the catastrophe of the Jewish people caused by Nazis and their aides" (Young 1990, 442). Many decades later, this commemorative event, which typically takes place in the spring, has expanded far beyond the borders of Israeli society to North American and European nations and communities. Today commemorative ceremonies are held in both secular and religious settings and are performed by Jews as well as by non-Jews.[1] In the United States, for example, Holocaust Remembrance Day is commemorated at national, state, and community levels. Writing on the history of *Yom Hashoah*, James Young offers this perspective on the evolution of Holocaust memorialization: "When conducted at civic centers or at public memorial sites, 'services' are as likely as not to be led by a rabbi or member of the religious community. In America, where the main organizing ideology is pluralism, ecumenical ceremonies bring together clergymen from diverse faiths and ethnic groups, Jewish survivors and Christian liberators. Each commemoration reflects the ethos and tradition, the piety or politics of a given community" (1990, 443).

Following Young's observations, the extent to which Holocaust Remembrance Day has become part of the cultural consciousness of the United States is indicative of the symbolic importance of Holocaust remembrance for the larger society, as presidents, members of Congress, and other elected officials frequently participate in the day's events. Beginning in the late 1970s and early 1980s, these events became marked by the inclusion of survivor testimonies. As the silence surrounding the atrocities and horror of the Holocaust began to dissipate, survivors became central actors in the construction of historical and cultural memory. Through the recitation of trauma narratives, the testimonies of survivors served to connect the audiences at Holocaust events to the suffering, loss, and victimhood of Jewish genocide (Connerton 1989), solidifying Holocaust remembrance within the "generation of memory" that has come to define the commemorative culture of contemporary society (Winter 2001). Since the 1990s a new form of trauma-carrying has emerged within this commemorative sphere. Increasingly, with the aging and loss of the survivor population, Holocaust remembrance, while continuing to proliferate (Flanzbaum 1999), has expanded to include the descendants of survivors who are either joining or replacing their parents and grandparents as social actors in commemoration ceremonies. In communities across the United States, Holocaust ceremonies now typically include descendants whose own stories have become intermingled with those of their parents and grandparents. This shift represents a changing culture of Holocaust memory in which carrier groups have been reconstituted and reinvented. To illustrate this trend in memorial culture, I draw on my research and fieldwork at synagogue and school events.

Holocaust Ceremonies and Descendant Testimonies

In numerous communities across North America and Europe, the observance of Holocaust Remembrance Day takes place within a synagogue setting. During my extensive years of fieldwork, I attended numerous synagogue ceremonies as a participant observer in a diverse number of geographic regions that included mid-sized and large urban centers. These events were typically sponsored by the Jewish community in collaboration with secular community organizations. In tracing the changes I observed over time, I found in my research a strong suggestion of the increasingly important social role that descendants have come to play in the creation of Holocaust memory. The first ceremony I attended more than a decade ago closely followed the structure of a commonly used interfaith service, *The Six Days of Destruction: Meditations Toward Hope*, that was developed by Elie Wiesel and Albert Friedlander in 1978. In keeping with the interfaith format, the service began with a meditation in which the importance of silence as a pathway to remembrance was invoked through the moral narrative of Nazi evil and human complicity: "Silence is the beginning of the reckoning of the soul, the prelude to an account of the past and the consideration of the present. May our shared silence lead us to awareness of a time of total evil that degraded our most precious values, the very meaning of religious existence, and life itself. Our silence is to be a committed accounting for other silences, that accepted persecutions and were indifferent to debasement and crime. For there *was* a time when silence was a crime." The meditation was then followed by the lighting of memorial candles, the reading of a testimony from a young boy's diary, and the recitation of Christian theological writings from across Europe.

A few years later, this same community, while still following the Wiesel and Freidlander model, restructured the service to include the oral testimonies of survivors who were invited to speak at the event. This change in commemorative practices dramatically altered the social context in which the Holocaust was remembered. The victims, now speaking for themselves, provided an emotional and identifactory link to Holocaust sufferance that over time and across cultures has emerged as perhaps the most powerful and effective means to convey the terror and criminality of genocide. In more recent years, the ceremonies have undergone further modifications, with extended family members now joining survivors at these public events. In place of a single survivor's story, the ceremonies have grown to include multigeneration testimonies that have further reframed the act of remembrance.

A case in point is that of a recent event in a mid-sized Jewish community that featured a dialogue among a small group of women survivors, their daughters, and their granddaughters. This approach signals yet another new direction in commemorative practices, focusing attention both on generational stories and on women as central actors in Holocaust remembrance. The rabbi who was leading the multigenerational ceremony began the evening by asking all of the survivors who were present to stand. Next he asked their children to stand and then their grandchildren. As each group was singled out and joined the others, the

Day of Remembrance was marked, from the outset, by a lineage-based rite of acknowledgment in which the descendants of survivors took their rightful place alongside their parents and grandparents as representatives of Holocaust trauma. During this ceremonial act of acknowledgment, audience members were visibly moved by the generational presentation. As the members of each generation rose to their feet, gasps and murmurs could be heard across the sanctuary as the mantle of survivorship passed from those who lived through the horrors of the Nazi regime to those who were charged with carrying the memories forward.

Following the identification of survivors and their families, a candle-lighting ceremony honored the six million Jews who had died in the Holocaust. Six survivors were then called to light one candle each for the six million victims. Once the candle lighting was completed, the reciting of Holocaust testimonies began. Three elderly survivors were asked to take their place in a circle of chairs in the front of the sanctuary. Once they were seated, their daughters and granddaughters were asked to join them. With the encouragement of the rabbi, each survivor took a turn in telling her story. The narratives, having never before been shared in a public setting, were conveyed through a variety of speaking styles and reflected the diversity of survivorship that characterizes Holocaust testimonies. Accordingly, one survivor described the violence of *Kristallnacht* (the Night of Broken Glass), another the deprivations of ghetto life, and a third the atrocities of concentration and death camps. After each survivor spoke, their daughters were then asked to reflect on what it was like to be a descendant of a survivor. Here, too, the accounts were varied. While all of the daughters spoke of the strength and survivorship of their mothers, they also revealed the struggles of a childhood in which they were sometimes lonely, in which fear and anxiety permeated the household, and in which the pressure for Jewish survival was palpable. When it was the granddaughters' turn to speak, they described their family legacy as both victimhood and resilience.

In the weeks following the ceremony, I interviewed a number of participants at the event. One of the daughters offered this account of her decision to join her mother on the "survivor panel": "When the rabbi asked me to do it, I realized that I have a story to tell, and my mother is ninety and who knows how long she will be here, and she wanted me to do it. So when the rabbi first asked he said please ask your siblings too, and I did and one sister said, tell him no, we all have PTSD [post-traumatic stress disorder]." Prior to this commemorative ceremony, the daughter had never spoken to groups or at community venues about her family or her mother's history. Because her siblings did not participate, she felt an obligation both to her mother and also to the Jewish community to speak openly and honestly about the suffering the Holocaust had caused and the tensions of her own traumatic inheritance. She described how the responsibility for carrying the memory of the Holocaust into the public sphere involved a competing set of obligations in which she felt both the need to be true to herself as a daughter of a survivor and, at the same time, to shield her mother from the pain that total honesty would bring. Here she explains the conflicted feelings that emerged following the presentation:

> You know, afterwards I was embarrassed because I said some things that sounded like that, you know, I didn't want to date Jewish boys and I was like, I can't believe you said that—you just said that out loud. I think I also said I just wanted to be me, not her, and that was a little embarrassing, and I felt selfish when I was saying it out loud. But, on the other hand, it was true. But I didn't know if it sounded hurtful. I didn't want it to be hurtful. And so I wasn't quite sure, if when I left and I was reflecting, I was hoping what I said wasn't hurtful.

Concerns over speaking out at Holocaust events were also expressed by other respondents who wrestled with their role of trauma carrier and the content of their message for a public discourse. Within this sample population specifically, first-generation descendants were especially concerned about the social meanings that their messages brought to Holocaust Remembrance Day. In their accounts, they discussed the tensions over the obligation to represent the travails of their parents and the equally significant responsibility to educate the public on the multigenerational effects of mass trauma, including the difficulties of growing up in survivor families. Thus, first-generation descendants were torn between telling their own stories as children of survivors (stories that frequently reveal the problematic familial dynamics of traumatic inheritance) and the obligation to honor publicly the suffering of their traumatized parents. When taking their message out of the synagogue ceremonies and into the secular arena, descendants further grappled with the emotional demands and tensions that emerge from their responsibility to represent the Holocaust, their own experiences, and the trauma of their parents' past.

Descendant Carrier Groups and Educational Settings

In addition to the synagogue as a place of Holocaust remembrance, secular venues such as public schools and universities have also become sites of commemoration for Holocaust remembrance. In comparison with synagogue commemorations, however, school programming reaches a broad constituency of young people of wide-ranging ages and backgrounds. Further, educational programs are frequently all-day or multi-day events that include films, speakers, and survivor testimonies that fall within a specified period of remembrance that may expand beyond Holocaust Remembrance Day to the observance of Holocaust Awareness Week. According to the respondents, participation in school commemorative events is especially meaningful because the school setting gives descendants the opportunity to teach future generations specifically about the Holocaust and the dangers of genocide. In choosing to assume the role of carrier in school programs, the descendants described a moral obligation that was often framed within a Jewish worldview. Here a respondent explains his commitment to the "broader message" of Holocaust remembrance: "Once you are the minority person, and your family was in pain and were annihilated then you think . . .

what's going on in places like Sudan is the same. One of the tenets of Judaism is the obligation to repair the world, so that's quite a legacy to believe in and to be a tenet of the religion. It's something I admire and respect and want to live up to."

In keeping with the scholarship on social consciousness among children of survivors (Berger 1997), the respondents expressed what has sometimes been described as a missionary zeal in their desire to keep the Holocaust in public consciousness, as one respondent reported: "I want to get out there and educate, not dwell on my own psychological problems, but to teach others the truth of what happened." Other participants expressed similar thoughts, describing this mission as "their work" and as an "obligation to carry the legacy and to speak up from our perspective." This phenomenon was particularly evident among respondents whose parents had recently died and whose memory they sought to sustain through assuming a more visible role in the culture of Holocaust representation. A fifty-five-year-old male respondent thus noted: "It's important that as the second generation [first-generation descendants] we speak, especially now because the first generation is dying. They're gone, almost. Five years, they'll all be gone. For me right now, today, I feel more passionate about what I carry than probably ever before. I'm also clearer about my responsibility than I have ever been."

In some instances, the descendants chose to become part of the public representation of the Holocaust to continue the work of a survivor parent. Here a fifty-four-year-old son who visited a death camp with his father expressed a desire to retire early and devote his time to "carry on what my dad was doing and go to spread the word." Another respondent whose father regularly spoke at Holocaust events made the decision to "take his place" once his father was no longer able to participate. His transition into the public carrier role, however, was not easy, as he relates here:

> I have spoken at schools twice. The first time, I had to sit down and prepare and say, "What am I gonna say?" It brings a lot to light, including the fact that I know nothing about it—I wasn't there. I can't give firsthand

experience. I grew up here. I played football and joined the Boy Scouts, trick-or-treated on Halloween. So I didn't know what I could tell these kids, other than I could present my father's story and then tell them about what happened when we went to Treblinka. You go to Treblinka now and it's like a park. . . . Somebody could say, "What are you talking about, there were gas chambers here? They buried people here? There's nothing here." It's just so easy to deny and people are so ignorant. How do you prove it? That's what I thought about before I spoke, how will I convince them?

As this account reveals, for descendant carrier groups the dilemma of authentic representation is compounded by the threat of Holocaust denial. Thus, both children and grandchildren of survivors seek to carry on the memory of their parents' trauma as a safeguard against forgetting and the erasure or denial of the past. A respondent in his early fifties recounted his first experience of representing his father's traumatic history at a school program. In the latter part of his father's life, a local university had produced a short video of his father's death camp survival. The film became the medium through which the respondent conveyed his father's past to schoolchildren:

I had some emotional difficulty that first time around. I'd seen the film of my father several times, but we sat there with these students, watching it, before we got up and spoke, and the whole thing about what I was doing affected me. So I got a little choked up that first time, had a little difficulty with it. But the weird thing is the last time we did it, I realized it became easier for me to do. Is that a good thing? No, to me it kind of illustrates the fact that terrible things, as they become further and further displaced, they affect you less, and I thought how easy it is, even though we still have a few survivors left in the world, and we have children of survivors, how it's already becoming easy for the president of Iran, let's say, to say it is a myth. That's something I was thinking about at the school last time. How do you show the truth?

Among grandchildren of survivors, the commitment to "tell the truth" was also significant. In one particularly moving account, a nineteen-year-old grandson created a photographic essay of the camp where his grandfather had been imprisoned. He described his visit to the camp as a "mission" to document the history of Nazi atrocities, a mission that culminated with the production of a slideshow that he presented to his youth group upon his return:

> It was tough, but it was something I had to do and I knew I wanted to do, not only for myself, but for my father, my grandparents. When I was at the camp, as much as it was hurting inside, I still felt it was important to take pictures, to document it. I knew it was important for my grandparents. When I came back, I waited a couple of weeks and then I put together a slideshow. I used music in the background, the *Schindler's List* soundtrack, adding the effect and the emotion coming in and all. . . . So I showed the slides at the event we have every year. It struck people, especially the guys who I knew were very tough. They started bawling like crazy, too. It was very powerful.

Similarly, a granddaughter of Israeli survivors recalled her role in a Holocaust program after returning from a school trip to sites of terror in eastern Europe. Here she recounts the emotional difficulties of representing the Holocaust and her sense of personal obligation to educate and to remember for the community:

> When we came back to Israel, it was very close to Holocaust Remembrance Day. There was a program at the *kibbutz* on Holocaust Remembrance Day and they asked me to read something. I was still emotionally drained from the trip but then I thought of my grandparents, all their relatives and all these Jews that died in the Holocaust and I knew I should do it. As the siren went off that day [to signal a moment of silence for Holocaust Remembrance Day], I felt myself going, like everything hit home. I was the first one to read and somehow I made it through the readings.

As these and other narratives illustrate, the role of carrying among descendants is often a difficult one, particularly in public settings where retelling a parent's or grandparent's trauma engenders deep emotions that, as described earlier, are heightened by the descendant's engagement with the past at sites of terror. In their role as public carriers, descendants are both the heirs to and recipients of survivor trauma and co-producers of traumatic memory for the larger society.

Further, first-generation descendants who participate in school events also report feeling conflicted about openly acknowledging the impact of survivor suffering on succeeding generations. In their roles as trauma agents within the school settings, these descendants, like those at the multigenerational synagogue commemorations, grapple with the obligation to recount their parents' tragic history and the competing responsibility to tell their own stories as descendants of historical tragedy. In resolving this dilemma, one respondent chose to represent the Holocaust as a cross-generational trauma in which the effects of posttraumatic stress disorder (PTSD) inevitably are passed down to the children and perhaps even to the grandchildren of survivors:

> When you are a second generation [first-generation descendant] growing up in a family where one or both of the members have been traumatized massively, and I use this example as I do in my presentations, we're not talking about 9/11, [when] 2,800 people died. Those people [the survivors of 9/11] will suffer consequences, PTSD for a couple of generations because of that. It's just what is going to be. I said on the panel that the Holocaust was six years and if you were German, twelve years. So there's this massive trauma daily for thousands and thousands of people. It is a very unique situation. And that is what I try to say.

Within the context of both synagogue and school commemorations, the shifting representations between survivor stories and descendant narratives reveal the tensions that confront carrier groups in their efforts to memorialize the past through the lens of intergenerational trauma. In bringing their personal accounts to the public sphere, descendants become carriers in two important ways: as recipients of the original trauma of the Holocaust and as individuals who experienced their own traumas as children of survivors. These generational tensions are perhaps most evident in the dissemination of descendant narratives through the production of art, literature, and film.

Carrier Generations and the Production of Cultural Memory

As the foregoing accounts suggest, Holocaust Remembrance Day provides an important social context for the transmission of trauma from the privatized sphere of the family to the public realm of Holocaust memorialization. As illustrated by the transformation in Holocaust ceremonies and school programming, descendants of survivors are rethinking the message of the Holocaust as they grapple with the impact of genocidal trauma on succeeding generations. This dynamic of Holocaust remembrance reflects the changing landscape of public representation that is also evident in the cultural production of Holocaust memorialization in film, art, and literature. Beginning with a discussion of descendant filmmaking, the significance of cultural production among children of survivors will be considered from the perspective of the varied creative processes by which personal and familial trauma enters into the public arena.

Filmmaking among Carrier Generations

The use of film as a medium of Holocaust-carrying is a widespread phenomenon, with a diverse range of representations that have been created and produced by children of survivors (Berger 1997; Stein 2014). Among the participants in this study, four respondents (three children and one grandchild of survivors) chose film as the medium through which their experiences as carriers were articulated for a wider audience. Within the descendant documentary film genre, "carrier" films tend to fall into one of two categories of filmmaking: those that celebrate the survival and hardships of their parents and grandparents and those that address the inheritance of trauma across generations. With respect to the first approach, that of preserving and telling the survivors' stories, one respondent produced an award-winning documentary film in which she returned to the rural area of France where her father, as a young German child, had been sent into hiding. The film was inspired by her father's recollections of the kindness and courage of the inhabitants of a French village whose teachers educated the hidden children and whose caretakers concealed them from the Nazi occupiers.

As a descendant narrative, the film reveals her father's history through interviews with survivors, village residents, and two sisters who were the village schoolteachers during France's occupation by Germany. According to the respondent, it was "a chance to make a beautiful film, different than films like *The Sorrow and the Pity* or *Night and Fog*, to present a different side." The respondent further explained: "I learned about his stories as a child. Our family was not like other Holocaust survivor families. We always talked about what happened to him and his family. He does not consider himself a survivor but I do [consider him a survivor]. The Holocaust is really central to my identity, and the film came out of that identity."

This centrality of the Holocaust to this descendant's identity provides the backdrop against which her film was made. Although she provides narration for the documentary, it is the survivors and the villagers whose voices are the strongest and whose memories frame the narrative of French resistance to the Nazis and the children's debt to the village. In the film, the respondent rarely speaks of herself except to say that her father frequently commented on her resemblance to his mother, a grandmother she never knew. Toward the end of the film, the descendant uses the documentary to convey her father's message and thus her own, that there is both good and evil in the world and that survivors and their children should always seek to do what is right. For this descendant, filmmaking became a path to social justice, representing the values of inclusivity and tolerance through the stories both of the children and their saviors.

By comparison, other descendant filmmakers have created a very different type of video presentation. Rather than focus on a parent's biography, these descendants tell their own unique stories as trauma carriers. Among the first of these films was *Breaking the Silence* (1984), a documentary that was developed more than thirty years ago. Produced by Eva Fogelman, a psychologist and child of survivors, the film draws on the experiences of members of a Children of Survivors group to explore the unique position and perspectives of first-generation descendants. Initially intended to facilitate and foster communication between children of survivors and their parents (Stein 2014), the video is currently available for educators and Holocaust programs. To this end, the film's website describes the video as "a healing encounter between two generations" and describes the documentary as "a moving story of personal growth as the children of Holocaust survivors find the strength to confront their painful legacy and overcome the barriers of unasked and unanswered questions that separate them from their parents. As the young adults connect with their parents, the second generation [children of survivors] discovers its own voice and grapples with the question of how to bear witness to their own children" (National Center for Jewish Film n.d.).

As a vehicle for the transmission of trauma to a wider audience, the film provides insight on the difficult family dynamics that shape descendant populations. Among the most important messages that this film conveys is the acknowledgment of an emotional divide that separates the child from the traumatized survivor and that remains a source of pain, confusion, and anger for the adult descendant. As a teaching tool and Holocaust lesson, the film highlights for the audience that the descendant story is a narrative of deep family bonds as each generation—the survivor parents and their children—confronts the rawness of Holocaust memories and the unmet needs of a generation that was born into the posttraumatic culture of Holocaust survivorship. What is perhaps most revealing about this film, especially in comparison with the intergenerational dialogues that more recently characterize Holocaust Remembrance Day, is the openness and candor with which the descendants address their parents on camera, in some cases angrily demanding answers and in others softly admonishing the survivors for withholding information. In this retelling of the trauma, it is not the survivors whose accounts are privileged but the descendants who are seeking to speak truthfully and to find a path toward healing through a filmed confrontation with a difficult childhood.

More than a decade after the making of *Breaking the Silence*, another support group for descendants sought a similar medium of communication to preserve and tell the generational story. Members of this group, many of whom participated in this study, were part of a Children of Survivors group that met regularly and that provided a basis for a collective identity of descendancy which informed their presentations at schools and other venues for Holocaust remembrance. Seeking to convey their message in a compelling format, the group chose documentary film. One member of the group, a videographer, offered this perspective on their decision:

> One of the women in the group, her son was on the committee for the local university's Holocaust Awareness Week. He asked his mom if our group would do a panel discussion. I think for the last year or two, different children of Holocaust survivors had gotten up and done panels. And the committee said, "You know we've done it this way for years, it's OK, but it's not the most interesting thing." Another member said, "Why don't we do something different? Why don't we have [. . .] make a video and then we could do a panel?" I said sure without even thinking. I didn't want to let everyone down and I said "Okay, let's do it."

Unlike *Breaking the Silence*, the documentary this group produced did not feature survivors. Although the participants often referred to and told their parents' stories, the film was conceived as an opportunity for descendants to reflect on their own lives and, as Robert Lifton has observed, to become part of a "social movement by children of survivors toward being heard" (quoted in Berger 1997, 144). A participant in her late forties explained: "For me it was fun doing the film but I wish I had talked more on the video, talked more about my emotional experiences so that more of my own story could be there. That was the good thing that came out of the film, giving us a chance to reflect on our lives in retrospect." In lending a sense of creativity and performance to the documentation of descendant narratives, the film became the venue for the expression of deep and previously unarticulated emotions (melancholy, sadness, and rage) that were enacted through storytelling, conversation, and poetry. As both a creative and biographical form of trauma-carrying, the descendants' video project is part of an expanding cultural field of Holocaust descendant art, literature, and memoir (Epstein 1979; Fremont 1999; Bukiet 2002; Hoffman 2004; Rosensaft 2014; Stein 2014), of which the work of Art Spiegelman is perhaps the most provocative and broadly disseminated.

The Graphic Artist as Memoirist and Trauma Carrier

The use of art and text as a medium for Holocaust-carrying is perhaps most strongly associated with the work of Art Spiegelman, the author of the graphic novels *Maus: A Survivor's Tale* (1986), *Maus II: A Survivor's Tale and Here My Troubles Began* (1992), and *Breakdowns: Portrait of the Artist as a Young Man* (2008). *Maus*, which began as a comic strip in the 1970s, has over time become a canonical if somewhat controversial text for Holocaust remembrance. Using animal graphics as representations in which the Jews are mice, the Nazis are cats, and the Poles are pigs, Spiegelman illustrates his parents' suffering and survival in a comic book style that provides a dramatic retelling of the Holocaust story through a deceptively childlike fable. Much has been written about *Maus* and Spiegelman's use of graphics and animal figures to tell "a survivor's tale" and his use of allegory to confront the larger meanings of the Holocaust—what it means to be human, to be racialized, and to enact evil (Berger 1997; Hirsch 1997). By comparison, much less attention has been paid to Spiegelman's representations of the relationship between father and son. In this respect, Hirsch writes: "On one level, *Maus* tells the story of Spiegelman's father, Vladek, from the 1930s in Poland to his liberation from Auschwitz in 1945; on another level, *Maus* recounts the story of father and son in 1980s Queens and the Catskills, the story of the father's testimony and the son's attempt to transmit the testimony in the comics genre which has become his profession, and the story of Art Spiegelman's life dominated by memories which are not his own" (1997, 26).

The descendant narrative, which occupies a small but important space within the graphic novel, is the story of a carrier who seeks to document, first by written account and then by audio recording, every possible detail of his family's travails. Woven throughout *Maus* is a son's desperate desire to record the "facts"—to get his father to speak and to remember, ostensibly for the book project that Spiegelman has begun. The subtext of the graphic novel, however, is that of multiple memories which document both the history of Holocaust victims and the experience of the damaged children of survivors.

As an example of trauma and its inheritance, the *Maus* chronicles offer an incomparable textual representation that, through the use of art and narrative, records both the suffering of the survivor father and the son's struggle to come to terms with his own rage, sadness, and loss. What is striking about Spiegelman's role in this representation of the Holocaust is the extent to which his work in recent years has become increasingly visible through the proliferation of documentaries on his life and work and through the growth of museum and gallery exhibitions. In 1991 the Museum of Modern Art in New York offered the first exhibit of the drawings and graphics of *Maus*, a show that was limited in scope and confined to a small lobby gallery in the museum. Twenty-three years later, in 2014, a much larger exhibition, entitled *Art Spiegelman's Co-mix: A Retrospective*, opened at the Jewish Museum in New York, following shows at the Pompidou Center in Paris and the Museum Ludwig Gallery in Cologne. This revitalized interest in Spiegelman indicates a turn toward Holocaust remembrance in which the descendant's life has begun to replace that of the survivor in the representation of Holocaust memory. The findings from my fieldwork and participant observation at the 2014 museum exhibit at the New York Jewish Museum illuminates the significant role of descendant art in conveying the meaning of traumatic inheritance within public spaces.

While the *Co-Mix* exhibition traced Spiegelman's artistic career over a five-decade period, including his beginnings in underground comics, the most provocative installations were those that focused on Spiegelman's childhood fears, his guilt, and his troubled relationships with his parents. It was these exhibits that tended to draw the largest crowds and that evoked the deepest emotional responses. Visitors were drawn especially to three installations that stood out for their representation of the intergenerational transmission of trauma within the Spiegelman family. The first group of comic panels, "Li'l Pitcher" (*Breakdowns 2008*), began with the image of Spiegelman as a little boy, sitting between his parents in a car ride home from a "fancy affair." Thinking that their son is asleep, Spiegelman's parents begin to talk about one of the guests who was a *Sonderkommando* at Auschwitz and with whom none of the other guests wanted to sit. Spiegelman, now awake, asks his father why no one wanted to sit with the man. His father answers that "in Auschwitz he threw Jews into the ovens . . . but it's [rumored] he put to the ovens his wife and his son." In the next panel, his mother tells Spiegelman to go back to sleep, his cartoon-like eyes wide open as he rests his head on her shoulder.

The second series of panels included comic illustrations from the work "Prisoner on the Hell Planet: A Case History," which is included both in *Maus* (1986) and *Breakdowns* (2008). These enlarged black-and-white graphics began with a portrait of the twenty-year-old Spiegelman in a striped prison uniform who returns home to find a crowd of people standing in front of his house in Queens. The succeeding panels show Spiegelman's learning of his mother's suicide, his emotional shock, and his caretaking of his devastated father. Through comic graphics, Spiegelman depicts his mother's funeral; his father's distraught behavior in the funeral chapel; and images of himself, wracked by guilt over his mother's death. The comic strip ends with a drawing of Spiegelman in prison, congratulating his mother for committing "the perfect crime. . . . You murdered me, Mommy, and you left me here to take the rap!!!"

The third comic series in which large numbers of visitors showed interest included a frame of images that brought the narrative of trauma-carrying to the second generation of descendants. This series, entitled, "A Father's Guiding Hand," begins with a haunting image of a large mouse-like figure hovering behind a tombstone. In the foreground a death-like hand emerges from the gray earth. What follows is a comic narrative that features a father offering a present to his son, a locked treasure box that was a gift from his father. As his son unlocks the box, a small monster is set free. The illustrated story continues with the fire-breathing monster growing larger and more frightening, his tongue bearing the head of a cartoon-like Hitler. In the last panel, the father, his tongue hanging out, has put the monster back in the box, while his son sits, head in hands, his clothes singed by this encounter with a terrifying past. The father then speaks through the comic bubble, telling his traumatized child that "you'll be able to pass it on to your son!" (2008).

Taken together, these three installations, each of which drew a large number of visitors, are powerful visual narratives that, with words and pictures, convey the impact of inherited trauma on successive generations. As many other scholars have documented, Spiegelman chose an outsider form of art and storytelling to represent and make public the burden of carrier generations. Although all of these pictorial narratives are found in his published books, the exhibit allows for a different and perhaps more riveting engagement with Spiegelman's story, as selected panels were shown separately and thereby highlighted and accentuated the images of a monstrous past. To judge by the strong emotional responses among the visitors to the exhibit, it was clear that the museum retrospective, in exposing the painful effects of intergenerational trauma, expanded the public representation of traumatic transference beyond the more traditional portrayals that characterize Holocaust commemoration.

The use of art and text to commemorate the Holocaust, while recognized as an important visual tool for cultural identification with Jewish genocide, remains (with the exception of Spiegelman) an understudied field of trauma representation and transmission. A review of the literature in the field focuses primarily on the multitude of studies that look to Spiegelman's images for the troubling and graphic visualizations of the Holocaust, as imagined by descendants (Staub 1995; Young 1998). While other research focuses on a small number of photographic artists whose work also has its roots in their descendant origins (Hirsch 1997; Zelizer 2001; van Alphen 2005, 2006), these studies, although important, do not fully examine the extent to which the larger field of visual culture has become a vehicle for carrying and conveying genocidal trauma to future generations. To further explore this dynamic of cultural production, the research now turns to the creation of Holocaust-themed art among the participants in this study.

Trauma-Carrying and the Production of Descendant Art

Four respondents (three children and one grandchild) chose art as the medium through which to express the intergenerational transmission of trauma. These respondents are part of a larger cultural trend in which both survivors and their descendants use art to capture and represent the social meanings and history of the Holocaust. While the work of survivor artists is often explained as the need to archive, with visual texts, the atrocities of their own past as well as those of others who did not survive, the art of descendants is frequently interpreted as a space of visual creativity where imagined horrors converge with the inner life of trauma carriers (Hirsch 1996; Laub and Auerhahan 1984). As a result, the production of art forms among descendants brings together the intergenerational transmission of trauma with personal and thought-provoking creative expression. To examine the importance of art to carrier generations, my analysis centers on the case of a fifty-eight-year-old respondent whose contemporary work has become focused on three Holocaust-related themes: her parents' traumatic histories in German slave labor camps, the agonies of torture and death, and postwar life in a refugee camp. To achieve her artistic goals as a carrier of Holocaust trauma, the descendant has taken a multimedia approach that incorporates photographs, material culture, painting, and artifacts. At the time of the research, the respondent was preparing for an exhibit of her Holocaust-related art. Thus, her studio provided a visual backdrop for the narrative content of her upcoming exhibition.

Further, it is significant to note that this respondent's art, which will be discussed in greater detail below, offers a unique view of Holocaust-carrying in that her parents were among the non-Jewish victims who were deported from eastern Europe by the Germans. Thus, in seeking out an understanding of herself and her work as a descendant of a survivor culture, she strongly identified with Jewish children of Holocaust survivors, while recognizing that her generational link to the descendant community was also informed by her outsider status as a non-Jew. Nevertheless, she sees her work as carrying on the memories and traumas of the Holocaust as they are represented by her parents' suffering and her own socio-emotional inheritance of a traumatic past.

My analysis of her work as artist/carrier begins with a discussion of the deportation and incarceration images in which she used photographs to memorialize her family history. This work includes two large collages that focus on her parents' deportation. One collage features her young mother as a deportee and the other collage depicts her father as a laborer. The collages consist of imagery from her parents' prisoner identity cards and reproductions of the head shot photographs that were taken by the Nazis when each parent entered the labor camp. Alongside these collages is a second photograph of her father. A closer look at the picture reveals Nazi symbolism that the artist has superimposed onto her father's face. Lightly covering her father's forehead and nose are the head, wings, and talons of the eagle that symbolized the Third Reich, her father's strong features blurred by the image of the eagle's body. With this imagery, the descendant has created a visual memory of a parent whose life was transformed by the trauma of incarceration and slave labor. In using this artistically rendered photographic portrait of her father, the artist represents two significant forms of memorial realism: the portrait of her father as a young deportee and his transformation by the "imprint" of Nazi terror that shaped both his and his daughter's life in the aftermath of war and genocide.

In a second set of art works, the respondent used painting to portray the horrors that filled her nightmares as a child and that still haunt her dreams now: "A lot of my work is based on dreams. The dreams are all nightmares and they all have to do with family history. I do dream about barbed wire a lot. One of the ones I have is, my brother and I are each wrapped with barbed wire. We are trying to reach each other. Our hands are cut. The hands are trying to go through, to connect, and we can't touch because of the pain we are experiencing from the barbed wire." The images from this dream have been incorporated into a graphic portrayal of torture and suffering that shows the naked bodies of women and men who, writhing in agony, are tied to one another by wire fencing that immobilizes them. Like the work of Spiegelman, these paintings in particular make visible to the outside world the interior suffering and pain of descendant generations.

In another series of related pictures that have emerged from the descendant's dreamscapes, flowers are used to symbolize a cycle of life, decay, and death. For this work, the respondent scanned natural flowers onto a large sheet of paper, creating a still-life with one living flower and another still-life with a decomposing flower. Here she describes the meaning of her work: "So one flower is in the process of dying and one is alive. So I find the beauty in the death which is so terrifying to me. So if I can find the beauty then death is really not that awful. I have two series here, one more abstract and one which is for me reality. Here the flowers are starting to bloom, to give life, and there the other is the process of dying. No matter what I do, death comes into it somehow."

The final theme of this respondent's art is that of a postwar family history in which the tragedy of the Holocaust is set against life in a refugee camp in Germany. For this exhibit, the descendant returns to photographic representations, selecting photographs of her parents, her sister, and herself as a young family living in the refugee camp and awaiting asylum. In one photograph, a young, smiling mother holds a child (the respondent) in her arms while another child, an older daughter, clings to her mother's skirt. In another photograph, her father sits with other refugees, serious men who unsmilingly face the camera. Enlarged to many times their original size, these images are the centerpiece of a sizeable installation that conveys both the solemnity of the formerly victimized men and the domesticity and motherhood of the formerly captive women. With these photographs, the descendant is contributing to the archive of Holocaust photography that, according to Hirsch, is distinguished by "ordinary snapshots and portraits, family pictures" that give context and humanity to Holocaust memory (Hirsch 1997, 20). Taken together, the descendant's artistic work is emblematic of a carrier generation that, through multiple media and narrative texts, tells the survivors' stories while also revealing their own inner life as the culture bearers of a traumatic and unforgotten past.

In demonstrating the diverse forms of social and cultural expression that descendants use to represent the Holocaust, this chapter highlights the significant role that carrier groups play in the transmission of historical trauma to the wider society (Alexander 2004a). Through personal testimony, documentary filmmaking, writing, and graphic and representational art, descendants bring to public consciousness the meaning of genocide for past, present, and future generations. In looking toward the growing importance of trauma-carrying among children and grandchildren of survivors, the Conclusion brings together the findings of the book with an analysis of the changing nature of Holocaust memorialization among both survivors and their descendants.

Conclusion

The Changing Landscape of Holocaust Remembrance and Future Directions in the Study of Traumatic Inheritance

Throughout this book the research has shown that the intergenerational transmission of Holocaust trauma is complicated and multifaceted. To a large extent, the expansive psychological literature in this field has shaped the way in which descendant populations are constructed in popular culture and defined by the scholarly community. In the vast majority of the existing research, descendants are portrayed as members of successor generations who have been wounded by the conscious and unconscious transfer of Holocaust loss and suffering. Although elements of this interpretative framework are found in the findings that have been presented here, the examination of the social structures of traumatic transference provides alternative perspectives through which to view the social inheritance of genocidal trauma and the creation of selfhood and carrier-group identity among children and grandchildren of survivors.

Taking as a starting point the family as the socio-cultural setting in which trauma is conveyed across generations, the research illuminates the role of narrative in shaping descendant selfhood and in connecting descendants to a terrible past. According to Ron Eyerman, it is through narrative and discourse that the past "is recounted, understood and interpreted through language and through dialogue" (2004, 162). In the case of Holocaust descendants, the children and grandchildren of survivors draw on multiple "founding stories" in which the past is evoked to create identities of victimhood, heroism, and moral agency. The past, then, as conveyed through narrative, becomes a frame of reference for the construction of a descendant self that is tied to the social and historical conditions of physical and cultural annihilation.

Narratives of traumatic histories, however, provide only one social mechanism through which the past is imparted, felt, and relived. As this research confirms, rituals are also instrumental in transmitting trauma and in influencing the development of the descendant self through the preservation and reinvention of tradition. As a space of emotional exchange and emotional distancing, ritual functions both as a vehicle for cultural persistence and as a site of cultural innovation within the historical framework of a genocidal legacy. Like narrative, ritual practices are part of the "cultural tool kit" (Swidler 1986; Wertsch 2002) from which descendants draw in constructing identities that are embedded in the past and that at the same time offer the possibility of separation from a tragic legacy.

In addition to ritual practices, descendants also turn to the spiritual realm to develop and sustain an individuated and separate sense of self. Here the research points to the ways in which descendants reject the religious beliefs of their ancestors even while they seek a spiritual orientation that can help to mitigate the despair of traumatic inheritance. In resisting a nihilistic worldview, descendants turn away from both theodicy and religious orthodoxy, choosing instead alternative spiritual paradigms that are individualistic and life affirming and that transcend the material realities of human suffering. Taken together, narrative, ritual, and spirituality constitute the interactive social and cultural frameworks that characterize the intergenerational transmission of trauma and contribute to the formation of descendant identity.

Further, the social dynamics of traumatic transference are also informed by the strains of familial attachment, the significance of extended kinship ties, and the importance of place as a source of identification and belonging. While previous work has pointed out the conflicts and tensions that arise within survivor families, the research that has been presented here reveals the tensions that emerge specifically over Jewish constancy and the attending fears surrounding intermarriage and "outsider" social relationships. This analysis helps to frame the social discord that has been found in survivor families within the threat of cultural and religious annihilation that is a legacy of genocidal trauma.

Moreover, the research brings a more nuanced understanding to the findings on family dysfunction and unresolved strain that tend to dominate the prevailing studies of the intergenerational transmission of Holocaust trauma. Perhaps because so much of the earlier work in this area was done on postwar adolescents in Israel or retrospectively on descendants coming of age in the 1970s and 1980s in North America, many of these studies focus on children of survivors who had not yet resolved the difficulties of a postwar childhood. By contrast, this study brings a more contemporary perspective to the relational world of survivor families. With the passage of time and the aging of both survivors and their descendants, the accounts reflect a longing for reparation and healing. This shift in the relational quality of familial ties points to the impact of age and generational transformation on descendant populations whose compassion for and admiration of survivors appears to grow and deepen over time. The intergenerational transmission of trauma therefore should not be treated as a fixed or stagnant stage of development. Rather, the process of traumatic transference is better understood as an ongoing dynamic of integration, reidentification, and reattachment in which succeeding generations continually negotiate and strengthen the bonds of kinship with survivors and their pasts.

Within this evolving social landscape of descendant connectivity, the findings also highlight the meaning and relational value of place. Because the trauma of genocide is also the trauma of exile and displacement, descendants express a sense of alienation and disconnection that mirrors the social dislocation of refugee survivors. Having inherited the sensibilities of the outsider, descendants often adopt a notion of home that is rooted in a European and eastern European imaginary of prewar life and culture to which they seek to return. These imagined places of cultural and emotional connectivity are envisioned as familiar, welcoming, and a source of national and even ethnic identity. Finding one's place in the aftermath of genocidal trauma therefore leads descendants back to the countries and geographies in which the tragedy of their families took place. In their search for home, later generations look to these cultural and geographic terrains for a sense of rootedness and belonging that has yet to be realized.

Beyond the promise of an ancestral homeland, the prewar topographies of Europe and eastern Europe are also marked by sites of terror to which descendants are drawn and that, like the survivors' countries of origin, have become part of the descendant imaginary. Through immersion in the geographies of suffering and fear, descendant identity is again reshaped, redefined, and reconstructed through ties both to survivors and to the sites of terror that have inhabited the dreams and fantasies of the children and grandchildren of survivors. The multiple landscapes of memory and imagined history—those that are associated with home and those that signify human cruelty and death—reveal how place functions as a legacy of genocidal trauma in the construction of descendant selfhood and in the emotional realm of connectivity. Along with narrative, ritual, belief, and kinship ties, place represents yet another social context from which carrier groups emerge to become social actors in the preservation and remembrance of a terrible past.

As the traumas of survivors are situated in the socio-biography of their children and grandchildren, many descendants turn to the public realm to carry the message of their family trauma into the larger cultural discourse on the Holocaust. In some instances, as in the creation of films and panel presentations, a collective identity of descendancy is portrayed. In other cases, descendants and their families assume a more individualized stance, speaking only for themselves and referring to events and worldviews that are defined by a specific survivor history. Whether as individuals or collectivities, descendant carriers have assumed a prominent role in Holocaust memorialization, and, as such, their participation in the public discourse has contributed to the changing dialogue of commemorative culture.

Holocaust-Carrying into the Future: Universalism versus Particularism

In his work *on perpetrator trauma*, Bernhard Giesen (2004) discusses the ways in which the Holocaust has been universalized and decontextualized from the specifically Jewish or German meanings of this horrific past. In this regard, Giesen writes: "Today, the Holocaust has acquired the position of a free-floating myth or a cultural icon of horror and inhumanity. . . . It is not a particularly German problem any more; every person can refer to it regardless of his or her origin, history, or descent, and it is understood by every member of a worldwide audience. . . . Independent of individual memories and recollections, of collective trauma and personal guilt, the Holocaust has ascended to the status of an undisputed master narrative" (2004, 142–43).

Although Giesen posits the development of a modern-day Holocaust iconography that has been removed and extracted from the historical origins of Jewish genocide, the acts and motivations of descendant carrier groups complicate this reading of the Holocaust. As the findings demonstrate, descendant carriers who situate their experiences and those of their parents and grandparents within a narrative of Jewish annihilation lay claim to this history as a distinctively Jewish tragedy and catastrophe. The descendants' personalization of historical trauma during remembrance ceremonies and events locates the meanings of the Holocaust within familial and ethno-religious frameworks that offer a less universal and more particular interpretation of the past.

At the same time, however, the findings also point to a growing trend among survivors and descendants in which acts of remembrance and representation have begun to "straddle the poles of universalism and particularism" (Levy and Sznaider 2006, 48). In an important turn toward what Daniel Levy and Natan Sznaider define as "cosmopolitism," a significant number of survivors and descendants have in recent years adopted a more global orientation toward Holocaust remembrance.

While the Holocaust, as the defining tragedy of the Jewish people, remains the "anchor memory" for the invocation of human suffering during these commemorative events, references to other modern-day genocides are often included and acknowledged in ceremonies that emphasize the persistence of persecution and mass violence across culture, time, and space. In these discourses, the Holocaust serves as the entry point to a universal acknowledgment of the evils and threat of genocide worldwide.

This turn away from the particular and toward the universal is exemplified by a recent Holocaust event that took place at a large metropolitan synagogue where I did participant observation in the last year of my research. The interfaith event was co-sponsored by the state government and the Jewish community. The list of presenters included clergy from diverse denominations, state and city officials, prominent Jewish leaders, Holocaust survivors, and descendants. The ceremony was held in the sanctuary of the synagogue with more than 500 people in attendance. In keeping with traditional Remembrance Day rituals, as described in the previous chapter, the commemoration began with an acknowledgment of the intergenerational link among survivors and their descendants. Accordingly, at the outset of the ceremony, survivors were asked to stand, followed by their children, their grandchildren, and finally their great-grandchildren. As the members of each group rose to their feet, they were loudly applauded, indicating the importance of each generation to the construction of a multigenerational context for the representation of Holocaust survivorship.

At the completion of the intergenerational ritual, the members of one family were brought up to the lectern to light a candelabrum that bore six candles for the six million Jews who died. During this stage of the ceremony, the survivor parent, who was recently deceased, was represented at the event by a video he had recorded just prior to his death, with the intention that it be played at the commemoration. As the members of his family waited to take their places on the dais, the image and voice of the survivor resonated throughout the sanctuary. In a posthumous narrative, the now-deceased survivor recounted his experiences during the Holocaust and the pride he felt in his children and grandchildren who would now carry on his legacy. At the end of the video, the survivor's spouse, children, and grandchildren came forward to light each one of the six memorial candles. This aspect of the ceremony introduced a new element to the performance of public remembrance, bringing together the spoken testimony of the deceased with the actions of the living descendants.

Following the candle-lighting ceremony, the commemorative event took a decided turn away from the particular and toward the more global. This shift was personified in the featured speaker, a child survivor who became a renowned judge in the international court system. During his presentation, the survivor first referred to his personal story of having been a prisoner in a number of different camps as a young boy, then moved the focus of his remarks to the late-twentieth-century war crimes tribunals and the importance of remembering the recent genocides in Africa and the Balkans. Here he reminded the audience that the Holocaust is not a singular event in history but is the memory through which all forms of mass violence and extermination must be considered and addressed. This survivor presentation embedded the recollection of the Holocaust in a dialogue on social justice, morality, and the persistence of genocide throughout the world. His perspective thus brought together two elements of contemporary Holocaust-carrying and memorialization: the representation of a specifically Jewish past and the moral obligation to invoke the Holocaust in the name of universal suffering and ethnic tragedy.

As evidenced by this present-day commemorative event, the intertwining of the particular with the universal has moved Holocaust remembrance toward a more global message. For a number of descendants in this study, this transition comes as a welcome addition to their carrier role. Seeking to balance the importance of Jewish memorialization with the moral imperatives of inclusivity, some descendant carriers have become mindful of the personal as well as universal meanings of Holocaust memorialization, as one participant strongly asserted: "We can't just tell our stories; we have to help others to see the connections between what happened to us and what is happening now. That is the Jewish face that the rest of the world has to see, that we as Jews care about others and want to put an end to genocide everywhere." Not only does this descendant understand the significance of his role in preserving the memory of Jewish trauma for the larger culture but, as cited here, he also assumes the responsibility for representing Jews more generally to the wider public. This dynamic of Holocaust-carrying points to the ways in which the cultural construction of the Jews in contemporary society is informed by the Holocaust. Because the image of the Jew in Western culture is often filtered through the memorialization and cultural production surrounding the genocide of World War II, carrier groups bear the responsibility for both portraying a traumatic past and for representing a group that continues to hold a marginalized position in society. The globalization of the Holocaust among descendant populations creates a narrative of inclusiveness and social conscience that shifts the public perception of the Jew from victim to moral advocate. In emphasizing an ethical commitment to social justice, members of Holocaust carrier groups are giving new meaning to the social value of collective recollections of the past that, when linked to the larger discourse on genocidal violence, contribute to the representation of universal Jewish values.

Beyond the Holocaust: The Intergenerational Transmission of Trauma and the Changing Character of Genocidal Legacies

Finally, in bringing this study to a close, I, too, like contemporary Holocaust carriers, look to the genocides of the late-twentieth and early-twenty-first centuries for the future direction of studies in the field of traumatic transmission. As the 1990s conflicts in Bosnia and Rwanda have come to represent the more recent forms of modern genocide, the research on the intergenerational transmission of trauma must look to these societies and cultures for a larger and more broad-based understanding of the social inheritance of genocidal histories. With respect to the study of traumatic transference, what distinguishes Bosnia and Rwanda from the Holocaust, among other differences, are two characteristics that specifically relate to postwar social struggles. The first characteristic relates to the postgenocide restoration of a divided nation. With the cessation of violence, perpetrators and victims in both Bosnia and Rwanda have been forced to live alongside one another in a "reunified" culture where the traumas of the past are everywhere in evidence.

In Rwanda, for example, legal policies have been put into place that prohibit the discussion or teaching of the past that references the conflict as an ethnically based narrative of Hutu perpetration and Tutsi victimization. In effort to create a national and unified consciousness, Rwanda has imposed a nationalist ideology on the postwar culture in which discussions of ethnicity as a dimension of the conflict have been suppressed (Purdekova 2008). By comparison, in Bosnia the visible divisions among the religio-ethnic groups in this Balkan country appear to have been intensified by the conflict, as Serbians, Croatians, and Bosnians each maintain ethno-nationalist narratives of the past in which the memory of Serbian genocide lies just beneath the surface of a tenuous peaceful coexistence (Powers 1996). Thus, in the movement toward reconciliation and national unity in Bosnia and Rwanda, the social relations of traumatic transference are deeply informed by the postgenocide social environments in which victims and perpetrators reside together.

In regard to the second differentiating characteristic of the Bosnian and Rwandan conflicts, the use of mass rape as a weapon of genocide has led to the birth of a large descendant generation whose traumatic inheritance has reproductive as well as socio-emotional implications. In both postgenocide cultures, rape victims and their children have been stigmatized by the dishonor of a mother's victimization and the disgrace of a child's birth. Further, these struggling families live in poverty and suffer the effects of displacement and dislocation as victims of sexual warfare (Erjavec and Volcic 2010). Although the intergenerational transmission of rape trauma is not unique to Bosnia and Rwanda, the magnitude of the victim populations and the expansion of this type of violence against women and children in modern-day genocides has transformed the way in which the trauma of mass violence is gendered and reproduced across generations.[1]

While the Holocaust provides a model for recognizing and establishing a field of study for the investigation into intergenerational phenomena, the more recent conflicts in Europe and Africa require a different sociological lens through which to analyze and consider the ways in which trauma is passed down from one generation to the next and the social meanings of this process. Future studies must therefore look to the social environment of postgenocide nations to provide a more comprehensive understanding of the social relations of victim/perpetrator coexistence and the effects of sexual violence on descendants who bear both the psychological scars of a parent's suffering and the isolation and alienation of children born of genocidal rape. As warfare and genocide continue to produce survivors of atrocity and incomprehensible loss, the children and grandchildren of traumatized populations will continue to bear the pain and suffering of their families' pasts. The work that has been presented here lays the foundation for addressing the interplay among emotion and social behavior, psychic injury, and the social dynamics of traumatic inheritance. It is clear from this research that to understand the depth and complexity of traumatic transference, scholars must address the social as well as psychological consequences of historical violence and the role of genocide in the destruction and re-creation of human societies across generations.

NOTES

CHAPTER 4. THE SOCIAL RELATIONS OF INHERITED TRAUMA
1 According to Jewish law, weddings cannot take place until after sundown on the Sabbath.

CHAPTER 6. DESCENDANTS AS HOLOCAUST CARRIERS
1 In Britain, Germany, and Spain, Holocaust International Remembrance Day is commemorated on January 27, the anniversary of the liberation of Auschwitz-Birkenau. In the United States this date has also been incorporated in some communities as a remembrance day, although the spring commemorative event is more commonly observed across the country. See Schnetter, Baer, and Rabl (2015).

CONCLUSION
1 The statistics on rape suggest that in Bosnia as many as 50,000 women may have been assaulted and in Rwanda as many as 200,000 women.

BIBLIOGRAPHY

Adler, Rachel. 1998. *Engendering Judaism: An Inclusive Theory and Ethics*. Philadelphia: The Jewish Publication Society.
Alexander, Jeffrey. 2004a. "Toward a Theory of Cultural Trauma." In *Cultural Trauma and Collective Identity*, edited by J. Alexander, R. Eyerman, B. Giesen, N. Smelser, and P. Sztompka, 1–30. Berkeley: Univesity of California Press.
Alexander, Jeffrey. 2004b. "On the Social Construction of Moral Universals: The 'Holocaust' from War Crime to Trauma Drama." In *Cultural Trauma and Collective Identity*, edited by J. Alexander, R. Eyerman, B. Giesen, N. Smelser, and P. Sztompka, 1–30. Berkeley: University of California Press.
Balakian, Peter. 2009. *Black Dog of Fate*. New York: Basic Books.
Baranowksy, Anna B., Marta Young, Sue Johnson-Douglas, Lyn William-Keeler, and Michael McCarrey. 1998. "PTSD Transmission: A Review of Secondary Traumatization in Holocaust Survivor Families." *Canadian Psychology* 39:247–56.
Barocas, Harvey. 1984. "Discussion of 'Children of the Holocaust and Their Children's Children: Working through Current Trauma in the Psychotherapeutic Process,' by Terez Virag." *Dynamic Psychotherapy* 2(1):61–63.
Bar-On, Dan. 1993. "First Encounter Between Children of Survivors and Children of Perpetrators of the Holocaust." *Journal of Humanistic Psychology* 33:6–14.
Bar-On, Dan. 1995. *Fear and Hope: Three Generations of the Holocaust*. Cambridge, Mass.: Harvard University Press.
Bar-On, Dan, Jeanette Eland, Rolf Kleber, Robert Krell, Yael Moore, Abraham Sagi, Erin Soriano, Peter Suedfeld, Peter G. van der Velden, and Marinus H. van IJzendoorn. 1998. "Multigenerational Perspectives on Coping with the Holocaust Experience: An Attachment Perspective for Understanding the Development Sequelae of Trauma Across Generations." *International Journal of Behavioral Development* 22(2):315–38.
Baron, Lisa, Howard Eisman, Michael Scuello, Alvera Veyzer, and Michael Lieberman. 1996. "Stress Resilience, Locus of Control, and Religion in Children of Holocaust Victims." *Journal of Psychology* 130:513–25.
Bartmanski, Dominik, and Ron Eyerman. 2011. "Trauma Construction and Moral Restriction: The Worst Was the Silence: The Unfinished Drama of the Katyn Massacre." Iin *Narrating Trauma on the Impact of Collective Memory*, edited by R. Eyerman, J. Alexander, and E. Breese, 237–65. Boulder, Colo.: Paradigm.
Baumel, Judith T. 1999. "Women's Agency and Survival Strategies During the Holocaust." *Women's Studies International Forum* 22(3):329–47.

Beim, Aaron. "The Cognitive Aspects of Collective memory." *Symbolic Interaction* 30(2007):7–26.

Bellah, Robert. 1987. "Legitimation Processes in Politics and Religion." *Current Sociology* 34:89–99.

Berenbaum, Michael. 1990. *After Tragedy and Triumph*. Cambridge: Cambridge University Press.

Berger, Alan. 1997. *Children of Job: American Second-Generation Witnesses to the Holocaust*. Albany: State University of New York Press.

Berger, Alan, and Naomi Berger, eds. 2001. *Second Generation Voices: Reflections of Children of Holocaust Survivors and Perpetrators*. Syracuse, N.Y.: Syracuse University Press.

Berger, Peter. 1967. *The Sacred Canopy: Elements of a Sociological Theory of Religion*. Garden City, N.Y.: Doubleday.

Bergman, M. S., and M. E. Jucovy, eds. *Generations of the Holocaust*. New York: Basic Books, 1982.

Binder-Byrnes, K., T. Duvedevani, J. Schneider, M. Wainberg, and R. Yehuda. 1998. "Vulnerability to Posttraumatic Stress Disorder in Adult Offspring of Holocaust Survivors." *The American Journal of Psychiatry* 155:1163–71.

Bird, Frederick. 1995. "Family Rituals and Religion: A Functional Analysis of Jewish and Christian Family Ritual Practices." In *Ritual and Ethnic Identity: A Comparative Study of the Social Meaning of Liturgical Ritual in Synagogues*, edited by J. N. Lightstone and Frederick B. Bird. Ontario, Canada: Wilfrid Laurier University Press.

Blum, Harold. 2007. "Holocaust Trauma Reconstructed: Individual, Familial, and Social Trauma." *Psychoanalytic Psychology* 24(1):63–73.

Blumenthal, David. 1993. *Facing the Abusing God*. Lousiville, Ky.: Westminster John Knox Press.

Bourne, Jenny. 1987. "Homelands of the Mind: Jewish Feminism and Identity Politics." *Race & Class* 29:1–24.

Boyarin, Daniel, and Jonathan Boyarin, eds. 1997. *Jews and Other Differences: The New Jewish Cultural Studies*. Minneapolis: University of Minnesota Press.

Bradshaw, Matt, Christopher Ellison, and Kevin Flannelly. 2008. "Prayer, God Imagery, and Symptoms of Psychopathy." *Journal for the Scientific Study of Religion* 47(4):644–59.

Bukiet, Melvin, ed. 2002. *Nothing Makes You Free: Writings by Descendants of the Holocaust*. New York: Norton.

Burtonwood, Neil. 2002. "Holocaust Memorial Day in Schools—Context, Process and Content: A Review of the Research into Holocaust Education." *Educational Research* 44(1):69–82.

Carmil, Devora, and Shlomo Breznitz. 1991. "Personal Trauma and World View—Are Extremely Stressful Experiences Related to Political Attitudes, Religious Beliefs and Future Orientation?" *Journal of Traumatic Stress* 4:393–404.

Chaitin, Julia, and Shoshana Steinberg. 2008. "'You Should Know Better': Expressions of Empathy and Disregard Among Victims of Massive Social Trauma." *Journal of Aggression, Maltreatment & Trauma* 17(2):197–225.

Charme, Stuart. 2000. "Varieties of Authenticity in Contemporary Jewish Identity." *Jewish Social Studies* 6(2):133–55.

Chodorow, Nancy. 1978. *The Reproduction of Mothering*. Berkeley: University of California Press.

Christ, Carol. 1979. "Why Women Need the Goddess: Phenomenological, Psychological, and Political Reflections." In *Womanspirit Rising: A Feminist Reader in Religion*, edited by C. Christ and J. Plaskow, 273–87. Berkeley: University of California Press.

Climo, Jacob. 1990. "Transmitting Ethnic Identity through Oral Narratives." *Ethnic Groups* 8:163–79.

Cohen, Steven. 1980. "American Jewish Feminism: A Study in Conflicts and Compromises." *American Behavioral Scientist* 23:519–58.

Cohn-Sherbok, Dan. 1996. *God and the Holocaust*. Wiltshire: Cromwell Press.

Connerton, Paul. 1989. *How Societies Remember*. Cambridge: Cambridge University Press.

Daly, Mary. 1973. *Beyond God the Father: Toward a Philosophy of Women's Liberation*. Boston: Beacon Press.

Danieli, Yael. 2007. "Assessing Trauma Across Cultures from a Multigenerational Perspective." In *Cross Cultural Assessment of Psychological Trauma and PTSD*, edited by J. Wilson and C. So Kum Tang, 65–89. New York: Springer.

Davidman, Lynn. 1991. *Tradition in a Rootless World*. Berkeley: University of California Press.

Davidman, Lynn, and Susan Tenenbaum. 1994. "Toward a Feminist Sociology of American Jews." In *Feminist Perspectives on Jewish Studies*, edited by L. Davidman and S. Tenenbaum, 140–68. New Haven, Conn.: Yale University Press.

Davidson, Shamai. 1980. "The Clinical Effects of Massive Psychic Trauma in Families of Holocaust Survivors." *Journal of Marital and Family Therapy* 6(1):11–21.

DeGloma, Thomas. 2009. "Expanding Trauma through Space and Time: Mapping the Rhetorical Strategies of Trauma Carrier Groups." *Social Psychology Quarterly* 72(2):105–22.

De Graaf, Theo. 1975. "Pathological Patterns of Identification in Families of Survivors of the Holocaust." *Israel Annals of Psychiatry & Related Disciplines* 13:335–63.

Dufour, Lynn. 2000. "Sifting through Tradition: The Creation of Jewish Feminist Identities." *Journal for the Scientific Study of Religion* 39(1):90–106.

Durkheim, Emile. 2001. *The Elementary Forms of Religious Life*. New York: Oxford University Press.

Eisen, A. 1998. *Rethinking Modern Judaism*. Chicago: University of Chicago Press.

Epstein, Arthur. 1982. "Mental Phenomena Across Generations: The Holocaust." *Journal of American Academy of Psychoanalysis* 10(4):565–70.

Epstein, Helen. 1979. *Children of the Holocaust: Conversations with Sons and Daughters of Survivors*. New York: Penguin.

Erjavec, Karmen, and Zala Volcic. 2010. "Living with the Sins of Their Fathers: An Analysis of Self-representation of Adolescents Born of War Rape." *Journal of Adolescent Research*. 25:359–86.

Ewick, Patricia, and Susan Silbey. 1995. "Subversive Stories and Hegemonic Tales: Toward a Sociology of Narrative." *Law & Society Review* 29(2):197–226.

Fackenheim, Emile. 1972. *God's Presence in History: Jewish Affirmations and Philosophical Reflections*. New York: Harper Torch Books.

Falk, Marcia. 1989. "Notes on Composing New Blessings." In *Weaving the Visions: New Patterns in Feminist Spirituality*, edited by Judith Plaskow and Carol Christ. New York: HarperCollins.

Falk, Marcia. 1996. *The Book of Blessings: New Jewish Prayers for Daily Life, the Sabbath, and the New Moon Festival*. San Francisco: Harper.

Fine, Alan, and Aaron Beim. 2007. "Introduction: Interactionist Approaches to Collective Memory." *Symbolic Interaction* 30:1–5.

Fishman, Sylvia. 1989. "The Impact of Feminism on American Jewish Life." In *American Jewish Yearbook*, edited by David Singer and Ruth Seldin, 3–62. New York: The American Jewish Committee.

Flanzbaum, Hilene. 1999. "The Americanization of the Holocaust." *Journal of Genocide Research* 1(1):91–104.

Fogelman, Eva. 1988. "Intergenerational Group Therapy: Child Survivors of the Holocaust and Offspring of Survivors." *Psychoanalytic Review* 75:635–50.

Fogelman, Eva. 1998. "Impact on the Second and Third Generations." In *Children Surviving Persecution: An International Study of Trauma and Healing*, edited by Judith Kestenberg and Charlotte Kahn, 82–89. Santa Barbara, Calif.: Praeger.

Fonagy, Peter. 1999. "The Transgenerational Transmission of Holocaust Trauma." *Attachment and Human Development* 1:92–114.

Fossion, Pierre, Marie-Carmen Rejas, Laurent Servais, Isy Pelc, and Siegi Hirsch. 2003. "Family Approach with Grandchildren of Holocaust Survivors." *American Journal of Psychotherapy* 57:519–27.

Fox, Nicole. 2012. "'God Must Have Been Sleeping': Faith as an Obstacle and Resource for Rwandan Genocide Survivors in the United States." *Journal for the Scientific Study of Religion* 51(1):65–78.

Fremont, Helen. 1999. *After Long Silence*. New York: Delacorte Press.

Froese, Paul, and Christopher Bader. 2007. "God in America: Why Theology Is Not Simply the Concern of Philosophers." *Journal for the Scientific Study of Religion* 46(4):465–81.

Fuchs, Esther. 2004. "Exile, Daughterhood and Writing: Representing the Shoah as Personal Memory." In *Representing the Shoah for the Twenty-First Century*, edited by Ronit Lentin, 252–68. London: Berghahn.

Gay, Miriam, Jonah Fuchs, and Mordechai Blittner. 1974. "Characteristics of the Offspring of Holocaust Survivors in Israel." *Mental Health and Society* 1:302–12.
Geertz, Clifford. 1973. *The Interpretation of Cultures: Selected Essays*. New York: Basic Books.
Gerson, Judith M., and Diane L. Wolf, eds. 2007. *Sociology Confronts the Holocaust: Memories and Identities in Jewish Diasporas*. Durham, N.C.: Duke University Press.
Giesen, Bernhard. 2004. "The Trauma of Perpetrators: The Holocaust as the Traumatic Reference of German National Identity." In *Cultural Trauma and Collective Identity*, edited by J. Alexander, R. Eyerman, B. Giesen, N. Smelser, and P. Sztompka, 112–54. Berkeley: University of California Press.
Glaser, Barney, and Anselm Strauss. 1967. *The Discovery of Grounded Theory: Strategies for Qualitative Research*. Hawthorne, N.Y.: Aldine de Gruyter.
Goldberg, Michael. 1995. *Why Should Jews Survive?* New York: Oxford University Press.
Gomolin, Robin. 2004. "Ideological Artifacts in Social Science Research: The Case of Rachel and the Theory of Intergenerational Transmission of Trauma." *The Discourse of Sociological Practice* 6(1):23–30.
Gottschalk, Simon. 2003. "Reli(e)ving the Past: Emotion Work in the Holocaust's Second Generation." *Symbolic Interaction* 26:355–77.
Greene, Roberta. 2002. "Holocaust Survivors: A Study in Resilience." *Journal of Gerontological Social Work* 37(1):3–18.
Gross, Rita. 1979. "Female God Language in a Jewish Context," in *Womanspirit Rising: A Feminist Reader in Religion*, edited by C. Christ and J. Plaskow, 167–73. Berkeley: University of California Press.
Gubar, Susan. 2002. "Empathic Identification in Anne Michael's *Fugitive Pieces*: Masculinity and Poetry after Auschwitz. *Signs: A Journal of Women in Culture* 28:249–77.
Gubkin, Liora. 2007. *You Shall Tell your Children: Holocaust Memory in American Passover Ritual*. New Brunswick, N.J.: Rutgers University Press.
Hajkova, Anna. 2013. "Sexual Barter in Times of Genocide: Negotiating the Sexual Economy of the Theresienstadt Ghetto." *Signs* 38(3):503–33.
Halbwachs, Maurice. 1992. *On Collective Memory*, Chicago: University of Chicago Press.
Hass, Aaron. 1990. *In the Shadow of the Holocaust: The Second Generation*. Cambridge: Cambridge University Press.
Heller, David. 1982. "Themes of Culture and Ancestry Among Children of Concentration Camp Survivors." *Psychiatry* 45:247–61.
Herman, Judith. 1992. *Trauma and Recovery*. New York: Basic Books.
Hirsch, Marianne. 1996. "Past Lives: Postmemories in Exile." *Poetics Today* 17(4):659–86.
Hirsch, Marianne. 1997. *Family Frames: Photography Narrative and Postmemory*. Cambridge, Mass.: Harvard University Press.
Hirsch, Marianne. 2008. "The Generation of Postmemory." *Poetics Today* 29:104–28.

Hoffman, Eva. 2004. *After Such Knowledge: Memory, History, and the Legacy of the Holocaust*. New York: Public Affairs.
Holmes, Jeremy. 1999. "Ghosts in the Consulting Room: An Attachment Perspective on Intergenerational Transmission." *Attachment and Human Development* 1:115–31.
Hovannisian Richard, ed. 1986. *The Armenian Genocide in Perspective*. New Brunswick, N.J.: Transaction.
Irwin-Zarecka, Iwona. 1994. *Frames of Remembrance: The Dynamics of Collective Memory*. New Brunswick, N.J.: Transaction.
Jacobs, Steven. 1993. "Judaism and Christianity After Auschwitz." In *Contemporary Jewish Religious Responses to the Shoah*, edited by S. Jacobs. New York: University Press of America.
Jacobs, Steven. 1994. *Rethinking Jewish Faith: The Child of a Survivor Responds*. Albany: State University of New York Press.
Jordan, J., A. Kaplan, J. B. Miller, I. Stiver, and J. Surry. 1991. *Women's Growth in Connection*. New York: Guilford Press.
Kansteiner, Wulf. 2004. "Testing the Limits of Trauma: The Long-Term Psychological Effects of the Holocaust on Individuals and Collectives." *History of Human Sciences* 17:97–123.
Katz, Stephen. 2005. *The Impact of the Holocaust on Jewish Theology*. New York: New York University Press.
Kellerman, Natan P.F. 2001a. "Perceived Rearing Behavior in Children of Holocaust Survivors." *The Israel Journal of Psychiatry and Related Sciences* 38(1):58–68.
Kellerman, Natan P.F. 2001b. "Psychopathology in Children of Survivors: A Review of the Research Literature." *The Israel Journal of Psychiatry and Related Sciences* 38:36–46.
Kellerman, Natan P.F. 2001c. "The Long-Term Psychological Effects and Treatment of Holocaust Trauma." *Journal of Loss and Trauma* 6:197–218.
Kellerman, Natan P.F. 2001d. "Transmission of Holocaust Trauma: An Integrative View." *Psychiatry* 64:256–67.
Kestenberg, Judith. 1980. "Psychoanalyses of Children of Survivors from the Holocaust: Case Presentations and Assessment." *Journal of American Psychoanalytic Association* 28(4):775–804.
Kestenberg, Judith. 1998. "Adult Survivors, Child Survivors, and Children of Survivors." In *Children Surviving Persecution: An International Study of Trauma and Healing*, edited by Judith Kestenberg and Charlotte Kahn, 56–64. Santa Barbara, Calif.: Praeger.
Kestenberg, Judith, and Milton Kestenberg. 1980. "Psychoanalyses of Children of Survivors from the Nazi Persecution: The Continuing Struggle of Survivor Parents." *Victimology* 5:368–73.
Kidron, Carol A. 2003. "Surviving a Distant Past: A Case Study of the Cultural Construction of Trauma Descendent Identity." *Ethos* 31:513–44.

Koontz, Claudia. 1994. "Between Memory and Oblivion: Concentration Camps in German Memory." In *Commemorations: The Politics of National Memory*, edited by J. Gillis, 255–79. Princeton, N.J.: Princeton University Press.

Langer, Lawrence. 1991. *Holocaust Testimonies: The Ruins of Memory*. New Haven, Conn.: Yale University Press.

Laub, Dori, and Nanette Auerhahan. 1984. "Reverberations of Genocide: Its Expression in the Conscious and Unconscious of Post-Holocaust Generations." In *Psychoanalytic Reflections on the Holocaust*, edited by Steven Luel and Paul Marcus, 150–67. New York: KTAV.

Lawrence, Richard. 1997. "Measuring the Image of God: The God Image Inventory and the God Image Scales." *Journal of Psychology and Theology* 25(2):214–26.

Lentin, Ronit. 2000. *Israel and the Daughters of the Shoah: Reoccupying the Territories of Silence*. Oxford: Berghahn.

Lentin, Ronit. 2004. "Memory, Forgetting and Mourning Work: Deviant Narratives of Silence in the Gendered Relations Between Israeli Zionism and the Shoah." In *Representing the Shoah*, edited by Ronit Lentin, 60–76. London: Berghahn.

Lev-Wiesel, Rachel. 2007. "Intergenerational Transmission of Trauma across Three Generations: A Preliminary Study." *Qualitative Social Work* 6(1):75–94.

Lev-Wiesel, Rachel, and Marianne Amir. 2001. "Secondary Traumatic Stress, Psychological Distress, Sharing of Traumatic Reminisces and Marital Quality among Spouses of Holocaust Child Survivors." *Journal of Marital and Family Therapy* 27(4):433–44.

Levy, Daniel, and Natan Sznaider. 2006. *The Holocaust and Memory in the Global Age*. Philadelphia: Temple University Press.

Linden, R. Ruth. 1993. *Making Stories, Making Selves*. Columbus: Ohio University Press.

Luckmann, Thomas. 1990. "Shrinking Transcendence, Expanding Religion?" *Sociological Analysis* 50:127–38.

Marcus, P., and A. Rosenberg. 1988. "The Holocaust Survivor's Faith and Religious Behavior and Some Implications for Treatment." *Holocaust and Genocide Studies* 3:413–30.

Maybaum, Ignaz. 1965. *The Face of God After Auschwitz*. London: Polak and VanGennep.

McGuire, M. 1993. *Religion and the Social Context*. Belmont, Calif.: Wadsworth.

Miller, J. B. 1991. "The Development of Women's Sense of Self." *Women's Growth in Connection*, 11–26.

Milligan, Melinda. 2007. "Buildings as History: The Place of the Collective Memory in the Study of Historic Preservation." *Symbolic Interaction* 30:105–23.

Mintz, Alan. 2001. *Popular Culture and the Shaping of Holocaust Memory in America*. Seattle: University of Washington Press.

Morgan, Michael L. 2001. *Beyond Auschwitz: Post-Holocaust Jewish Thought in America*. Oxford: Oxford University Press.

Nadell, Pamela. 2010. "Encountering Jewish Feminism." In *Why Is America Different? American Jewry on Its 350th Anniversary*, edited by Steven T. Katz, 91–104. Lanham, Md.: University Press of America.
National Center for Jewish Film, N.d. *"Breaking the Silence: The Generation after the Holocaust."* www.jewishfilm.org.
Neusner, Jacob. 1973. "The Implications of the Holocaust." *The Journal of Religion* 53(3):293–308.
Nora, Pierre. 1989. "Between Memory and History: *Les Liex de Memoire.*" *Representations* 26:7–24.
Ochayon, Sheryl. 2012. "Commemoration in the Art of Holocaust Survivors." In the international school for Holocaust Studies e-newsletter for holocaust educators. http://www.yadvashem.org/yv/en/education/newsletter/26/main_article.asp.
Olick, Jeffrey K. 1999. "Collective Memory: The Two Cultures." *Sociological Theory* 17:33–48.
Olick, Jeffrey K., and Joyce Robbins. 1998. "Social Memory Studies: From 'Collective Memory' to the Historical Sociology of Mnemonic Practices." *Annual Review of Sociology* 24:105–40.
Olick, Jeffrey K., Vared Vinitsky-Seroussi, and Daniel Levy. 2011. "Introduction." In *The Collective Memory Reader*, edited by J. Olick, V. Vinitsky-Seroussi, and D. Levy, 3–62. New York: Oxford University Press.
Oliner, M. M. 1982. "Hysterical Features of Children of Survivors." In *Generations of the Holocaust*, edited by M. S. Bergman and M. E. Jucovy, 267–86. New York: Basic Books.
Peskowitz, Miriam, and Laura Levitt, eds. 1997. *Judaism Since Gender*. New York: Routledge.
Phillips, Russell. 1978. "Impact of Nazi Holocaust on Children of Survivors." *American Journal of Psychotherapy* 32(3):370–78.
Plaskow, Judith. 1990. *Standing Again at Sinai: Judaism from a Feminist Perspective*. New York: HarperCollins.
Powers, Gerald. 1996. "Religion, Conflict and Prospects for Peace in Bosnia, Croatia and Yugoslavia." *Journal of International Affairs*, 50:22–40.
Prince, Robert. 1985. *The Legacy of the Holocaust: Psychological Themes in the Second Generation*. Ann Arbor, Mich.: UMI Research Press.
Purdekova, Andrea. 2008. "Building a Nation in Rwanda? De-ethnicisation and Its Discontents." *Studies in Ethnicity and Nationalism* 8 (3):208–23.
Raphael, Melissa. 1998. "Postmodern Jewish Feminism and the Complexity of Alternative Religious Identities." *Nova Religion: The Journal of Alternative and Emergent Religions* 1(2):198–215.
Raphael, Melissa. 2003. *The Female Face of Auschwitz: A Jewish Feminist Theology of the Holocaust*. New York: Routledge.
Richardson, Laurel. 1990. "Narrative and Sociology." *Journal of Contemporary Ethnography* 19(1):116–35.

Ringelheim, Joan. 1997. "Genocide and Gender: A Split Memory." In *Gender & Catastrophe*, edited by Ronit Lentin, 18–35. London: Zed Books.
Roof, Wade C. 1993. *A Generation of Spiritual Seekers: The Spiritual Journeys of the Baby Boomers*. San Francisco: HarperCollins.
Roof, Wade C. 1999. *Spiritual Marketplace: Baby Boomers and the Remaking of American Religion*. Princeton, N.J.: Princeton University Press.
Roof, Wade C., and Jennifer Roof. 1984. "Review of the Polls: Images of God Among Americans." *Journal for the Scientific Study of Religion* 23(2):201–5.
Rosenman, Stanley. 1984. "Out of the Holocaust: Children as Scarred Souls and Tempered Redeemers." *The Journal of Psychohistory* 11(4):555–67.
Rosensaft, Menachem. 2001. "I Was Born in Bergen-Belsen." In *Second Generation Voices: Reflections of Children of Holocaust Survivors and Perpetrators*, edited by Alan Berger and Naomi Berger. Syracuse, N.Y.: Syracuse University Press.
Rosensaft, Menachem, ed. 2014. *God, Faith & Identity from the Ashes*. Woodstock, Vt.: Jewish Lights Publishing.
Rosenthal, Gabriele, ed. 1998. *The Holocaust in Three Generations: Families of Victims and Perpetrators of the Nazi Regime*. London: Cassell.
Rothberg, Michael. 2009. *Multidirectional Memory: Remembering the Holocaust in the Age of Decolonization*. Stanford, Calif.: Stanford University Press.
Rubenstein, Richard. 1992. *After Auschwitz: History, Theology, and Contemporary Judaism*. Baltimore: Johns Hopkins University Press.
Rustin, Stanley. 1980. "The Legacy Is Loss." *Journal of Contemporary Psychotherapy* 11(1):32–43.
Sagi-Schwartz, Abraham, Marinus van IJzendoorn, Klaus Grossmann, Tirtsa Joels, Karin Grossmann, Miri Scharf, Nina Koren-Karie, and Sarit Alkalay. 2003. "Attachment and Traumatic Stress in Female Holocaust Child Survivors and Their Daughters." *American Journal of Psychiatry* 160(6):1086–92.
Saxe, L., B. Phillips, C. Kadushin, G. Wright, and D. Parmer. 2006. *The 2005 Boston Community Survey: Preliminary Findings*. Boston: Steinhardt Foundation for Jewish Life.
Scheff, T. 1979. *Catharsis in Healing, Ritual, and Drama*. Berkeley: University of California Press.
Schnettler, Bernt, Alejandro Baer, and Mareln Rabl. 2015. "Videographic Analysis of Religious and Secular Rituals: Examples from a Study of the International Holocaust Remembrance Day." In *Seeing Religion: Toward a Visual Sociology of Religion*, edited by R. Williams, 137–56. New York: Routledge.
Schuman, Howard, and Jacqueline Scott. 1989. "Generations and Collective Memories." *American Sociological Review* 54:359–81.
Schwartz, Barry. 1982. "The Social Context of Commemoration: A Study of Collective Memory." *Social Forces* 61(2):374–401.
Sered, Susan. 2000. *What Makes Women Sick? Maternity, Modesty, and Militarism in Israeli Society*. Hanover, N.H.: Brandeis University Press.

Shabad, Peter. 1993. "Repetition and Incomplete Mourning: The Intergenerational Transmission of Traumatic Themes." *Psychoanalytic Psychology* 10(1):61–75.

Sicher, Efraim. 2001. "The Future of the Past: Countermemory and Postmemory in Contemporary American Post-Holocaust Narratives." *History and Memory* 12(2):56–91.

Silverman, Kadja. 1992. *Male Subjectivity at the Margins*. London: Routledge.

Somers, Margaret. 1994. "The Narrative Constitution of Identity: A Relational and Network Approach." *Theory and Society* 23:605–49.

Sorscher, N., and L. J. Cohen. 1997. "Trauma in Children of Holocaust Survivors: Transgenerational Effects." *American Journal of Orthopsychiatry* 67:493–500.

Spiegelman, Art. 1986. *Maus: A Survivor's Tale*. New York: Pantheon.

Spiegelman, Art. 1992. *Maus II: A Survivor's Tale and Here My Troubles Began*. New York: Pantheon.

Spiegelman, Art. 2008. *Breakdowns*. New York: Pantheon.

Spilka, Bernard, and D. N. Mcintosh. 1996. "Religion and Spirituality: The Known and the Unknown." Paper presentation, American Psychological Association annual conference.

Staub, Michael. 1995. "The Shoah Goes On and On: Remembrance and Representation in Art Spiegelman's Maus." *MELUS* 20(3):33–46.

Stein, Arlene. 2009a. "Trauma and Origins: Post Holocaust Genealogists and the Work of Memory." *Qualitative Sociology* 32:293–309.

Stein, Arlene. 2009b. "Feminism, Therapeutic Culture, and the Holocaust in the United States: The Second Generation Phenomenon." *Jewish Social Studies: History, Culture, Society* 16:27–53.

Stein, Arlene. 2014. *Reluctant Witnesses: Survivors, Their Children, and the Rise of Holocaust Consciousness*. Oxford: Oxford University Press.

Suedfeld, Peter. 2000. "Reverberations of the Holocaust Fifty Years Later: Psychology's Contributions to Understanding Persecution and Genocide [Presidential address]." *Canadian Psychology* 41(1):1–11.

Surrey, Janet. 1991. "The Self in Relation: A Theory of Women's Development." In *Women's Growth in Connection*, edited by J. Jordan, A. Kaplan, J. B. Miller, I. Stiver, and J. Surrey, 51–66. New York: Guilford.

Swidler, Ann. 1986. "Culture in Action: Symbols and Strategies." *American Sociological Review* 51:273–86.

Turner, Victor. 1969. *The Ritual Process*. Chicago: Aldine.

Umansky, Ellen. 1988. "Review Essay: Females, Feminists, and Feminism: A Review of Recent Literature on Jewish Feminism and the Creation of a Feminist Judaism." *Feminist Studies* 14(2):349–65.

Umansky, Ellen, and Dianne Ashton, eds. 1992. *Four Centuries of Jewish Women's Spirituality: A Sourcebook*. Boston: Beacon Press.

van Alphen, Ernst. 2005. *Art in Mind: How Contemporary Images Shape Thought*. Chicago: Chicago University Press.

van Alphen, Ernst. 2006. "Second-Generation Testimony, the Transmission of Trauma, and Postmemory." *Poetics Today* 27:473–88.

Virag, Terz. 1984. "Children of the Holocaust and Their Children's Children: Working through Current Trauma in the Psychotherapeutic Process." *Dynamic Psychotherapy* 2(1):47–59.

Vogel, Miriam. 1994. "Gender as a Factor in the Transgenerational Transmission of Trauma." *Women and Therapy* 15:35–47.

Wagner-Pacifici, Robin, and Barry Schwartz. 1991. "The Vietnam Memorial: Commemorating a Difficult Past." *American Journal of Sociology* 97:376–420.

Wardi, Dina. 1992. *Memorial Candles: Children of the Holocaust*. New York: Routledge.

Waxman, Mayer. 2000. "Traumatic Hand-Me-Downs: The Holocaust, Where Does It End?" *Families in Society* 81(1):59–64.

Webber, Jonathan. 2006. "Memory, Religion, and Conflict at Auschwitz: A Manifesto." In *Religion, Violence, Memory and Place*, edited by O. Baruch and J. Shawn Landres, 51–70. Bloomington: Indiana University Press.

Weber, Max. 1968. *Economy and Society: An Outline of Interpretive Sociology*. New York: Bedminster Press.

Weisel, Mindy, ed. 2000. *Daughters of Absence*. Sterling, Va.: Capitol Books.

Weiss, Micha, and Sima Weiss. 2000. "Second Generation to Holocaust Survivors: Enhanced Differentiation of Trauma Transmission." *American Journal of Psychotherapy* 54(3):372–85.

Wertheimer, Jack. 1989. "Recent Trends in American Judaism." In *American Jewish Yearbook*, edited by David Singer and Ruth Seldin, 63–162. New York: The American Jewish Committee.

Wertsch, James. 2002. *Voices of Collective Remembering*. Cambridge: Cambridge University Press.

Winter, Jay. 2001. "The Generation of Memory: Reflections on the 'Memory Boom' in Contemporary Historical Studies." *Canadian Military History* 10(3):57–66.

Wiseman, Hadas, Einat Metzl, and Jacques P. Barber. 2006. "Anger, Guilt, and Intergenerational Communication of Trauma in the Interpersonal Narratives of Second Generation Holocaust Survivors." *American Journal of Orthopsychiatry* 76(2):176–84.

Wuthnow, Robert. 1998. *After Heaven: Spirituality in America Since the 1950s*. Berkeley: University of California Press.

Young, James. 1990. "When a Day Remembers: A Performative History of Yom ha-Shoah." *History and Memory* 2(2):54–75.

Young, James. 1993. *The Texture of Memory: Holocaust Memorials and Meaning*. New Haven, Conn.: Yale University Press.

Young, James. 1998. "The Holocaust as Vicarious Past: Art Spiegelman's 'Maus' and the Afterimages of History." *Critical Inquiry* 24(3):666–99.

Zaidman, Nurit. 1996. "Variations of Jewish Feminism: The Traditional, Modern, and Postmodern Approaches." *Modern Judaism* 16(1):47–65.

Zelizer, Barbie, ed. 2001. *Visual Culture and the Holocaust*. New Brunswick, N.J.: Rutgers University Press.

Zertal, Idith. 2000. "From the People's Hall to the Wailing Wall: A Study in Memory, Fear and War." *Representations* 69: 96–126.

Zerubavel, Eviatar. 1996. "Social Memories: Steps to a Sociology of the Past." *Qualitative Sociology* 19:283–99.

Zerubavel, Eviatar. 2005. *Time Maps: Collective Memory and the Social Shape of the Past*. Chicago: University of Chicago Press.

Zimmerman, Miriam. 2012. "From Germany and Back Again in Three Generations: A Family Reclaims Its Heritage." *The Jewish Post and Opinion* 78(7):10–12.

Zinnbauer, B., K. Pargament, B. Cole, M. Rye, E. Butter, T. Belavich, K. Hipp, A. Scott, and Jill Kadar. 1997. "Religion and Spirituality: Unfuzzying the Fuzzy." *Journal for the Scientific Study of Religion* 36:549–64.

Zubrzycki, Genevieve. 2006. *The Crosses of Auschwitz: Nationalism and Religion in Post-Communist Poland*. Chicago: University of Chicago Press.

Zuckerman, Bruce, Zev Garber, Jeremy Schoenberg, and Lisa Ansell, eds. 2008. *The Impact of the Holocaust in America*. West Lafayette, Ind.: Purdue University Press.

INDEX

acts of remembrance at sites of terror, 120–124
agency, identities of, 30–34
agnostic Jews, 70
ancestral ties and memory work, 99–104, 151–152
anchor memory, 154
anxiety and fear experienced by descendants at sites of terror, 109–116
art, production of descendant, 144–147
Art Spiegelman's Co-mix: A Retrospective, 141–142
atrocity narratives. *See* trauma narratives
attachment and strain across generations, 83–86
Auschwitz: anxiety and fear experienced by descendants at, 109–110, 112; death of God proclaimed after, 73; descendants' acts of remembrance and empathic bonding at, 120–121; descendants keeping Sabbath, 56; extended family relations with survivors of, 93; heroism in, 31; intergenerational transmission of religious beliefs and, 69; liberation of, 9, 110; narratives about arrival in, 20–21; narratives about life in, 17, 18; sexual exchange in, 34–35, 37; sexual violence against women and girls in, 22; survivor guilt and, 46

Balkans, the, 61–62
Bar-On, Dan, 41
Beim, Aaron, 107
Bergen-Belsen, 56, 112, 121

Bird, Frederick, 42
Bosnia, 156–158
Breakdowns: Portrait of the Artist as a Young Man, 140, 142
Breaking the Silence, 138–140
bubbe, 75
Buddhism, 54, 76–77

carriers, Holocaust, 125–147, 152; filmmaking by, 136–140; future of, 153–156; generations and production of cultural memory, 136–144; graphic artists as, 140–144; groups and educational settings, 131–136; Holocaust ceremonies and descendant testimonies and, 127–131; Holocaust Remembrance Day and, 126–127; production of descendant art and trauma-carrying by, 144–147; universalism versus particularism and, 153–156
Catholicism, 26
ceremonies, Holocaust, 127–131
Chanukkah, 59
Children of Holocaust Survivors, 3, 6, 93, 138
Chodorow, Nancy, 51
cosmopolitanism, 153
cultural memory, production of, 136–144
culture-bearing by descendants, 59–63, 87

Day of Atonement. *See* Yom Kippur
death, attachment and connection of descendant with survivors, 95–99
demasculinized God, 79–82

descendants, Holocaust, 1–2; acts of mourning at sites of terror, 116–119; acts of remembrance at sites of terror, 120–124; ancestral ties, Holocaust outsider, and search for "home" among, 99–104, 151–152; anxiety and fear experienced at sites of terror, 109–116; attachment and connection with survivors beyond death, 95–99; attachment and strain across generations, 83–86; carrier groups and educational settings, 131–136; culture-bearing by, 59–63; as Holocaust carriers, 125–147; interviews of, 5–6; in kibbutz communities, 26–27; location of, 4; marriages and relationships of, 3–4, 88–91, 150–151; *mikveh* rites for, 58; religious repression and ritual connectivity among, 60–63; religious upbringing of, 4–5; as research participants, 2–7; same-sex relationships among, 89; social relationships with extended family members, 92–94, 150–151; tattooing grandparents' numbers on themselves, 91–92; testimonies at Holocaust ceremonies, 127–131; victimized identities among, 24–29. *See also* carriers, Holocaust; sites of terror/memorials and monuments

dialectic of trauma, 42

dreams and fantasies with inherited memories, 24

Durkheim, Emile, 41–42

Eastern religious ideologies, 72

educational settings, carrier groups and, 131–136

Eichmann, Adolf, 18, 20

emotion: exchange, ritual as site of, 50–53; ritual and posttraumatic, 41–49

empathic bonding and acts of remembrance at sites of terror, 120–124

Ewick, Patricia, 14

extended family, relations with, 92–94, 150–151

Eyerman, Ron, 149

Falk, Marcia, 73

"Father's Guiding Hand, A," 143

feminism: demasculinization of God and, 81; self-in-relation theory and, 50–53

feminized construction of the divine, 74–75

filmmaking among carrier generations, 136–140

Fogelman, Eva, 138

Friedlander, Albert, 127–128

Geertz, Clifford, 41–42

generation of memory, 127

genocides, recent, 156–158

Gerson, Judith, 102

Giesen, Bernhard, 153

Gilbert, Martin, 29

God: death of, proclaimed after Auschwitz, 73; demasculinized, 79–82; fear of, 66–68; imagery among postwar Jews, 80–81; redefining masculinized figure of, 68–72; survivors' anger toward, 44–45, 66–67

Gottschalk, Simon, 120

graphic artists are memoirists and trauma carriers, 140–144

Gubar, Susan, 78–79

guilt, survivor, 46

Hajkova, Anna, 36

Hass, Aaron, 42–44

Herman, Judith, 42

heroism, 29–34, 149; identities of agency and, 30–34; selfhood and, 31–32; of survivors, 33–34

Hirsch, Marianne, 23, 104, 123, 141

Hoffman, Eva, 95

Holocaust, study of, 1–2, 10–12; changing character of genocidal legacies and, 156–158; traumatic inheritance in, 7–10, 13–14, 41
Holocaust Remembrance Day, 126–127. *See also* carriers, Holocaust
Holocaust Testimonies: The Ruins of Memory, 29

identity/identities: of agency, 30–34; descendants forging separate, 53–58, 87; inherited memories and, 23–24; Jews and postwar, 99–104; merging between second-generation descendants and grandparents, 27–29; modern Jewish, 57–58; moral, 34–39; narrative and, 14–15; victimized, 21–29, 149
immanence, 72–78
individuated spirituality, 72–78
inherited memories, 23–24
intergenerational transfer of trauma. *See* traumatic inheritance
International Network of Children of Survivors, 74
I Was a Doctor in Auschwitz, 34–35

Jewish Museum (New York), 141–142
Jewish Post and Opinion, 102

Kabbalism, 74–75
Kellerman, Natan, 50
kibbutz communities, 26–27, 134
Kristallnacht, 129

Langer, Lawrence, 29–30
Levi, Primo, 29
Levy, Daniel, 153
Linden, Ruth, 16

Majdanek, 118–119
Male Subjectivity at the Margins, 78

marriages and relationships of descendants, 3–4, 88–91, 150–151
masculinized God figure, redefining of, 68–72
Maus: A Survivor's Tale, 140–141, 142
Maus II: A Survivor's Tale and Here My Troubles Began, 140
memorial candle, 25; anchor, 154
memory: generation of, 127; post-, 123; production of cultural, 136–144; schemata, 107; social, 108; work, 99–104
metanarratives, 14
mikveh rite, 58
Miller, Jean Baker, 51
mitzvot, 71
modes of telling, 15–19
moral choices, 29–30, 149; heroism and identities of agency and, 30–34; selfhood and, 31–32, 37–38
moral identities, 34–39
Museum Ludwig Gallery, 142
Museum of Modern Art, 141

narratives, family, 13–14, 149–150; of agency, 29; on camp life, 18; identity and, 14–15; narrator, modes of telling, and tropes of remembrance in, 15–19; as ongoing and repeated, 17–18; survivors acting out, 18–19; told at family dinners, 16–17; trauma narratives, 19–29
National Museum of Anthropology, 108
Night and Fog, 137
Nora, Pierre, 106
Numbered, 91

Olick, Jeffrey, 108

Passover, 55, 56–57, 59
Perl, Gisella, 34–35, 36
perpetrator trauma, 153
place, importance of, 151–152

Pompidou Center, 142
postmemory, 123
posttraumatic stress disorder (PTSD), 17, 130, 135
postwar Jewish communities, 99–104
"Prisoner on the Hell Planet: A Case History," 142

rape, 22, 35–36, 157–158. *See also* sexual exchange and survival
Raphael, Melissa, 79
religious beliefs, 44–45, 65; agnosticism and, 70; crisis of Jewish patriarchy and, 78–82; fear of God, 66–68; individuated spirituality and turn toward immanence in, 72–78; intergenerational transmission of, 66–68; redefining masculinized God figure and, 68–72. *See also* ritual
repression, religious, 60–63
Ringelheim, Joan, 35–36
ritual, 150; connectivity and religious repression among descendants, 60–63; culture-bearing among descendants, 59–63; descendants' reinvention of, 53–58; as site of emotional exchange, 50–53; as site of posttraumatic emotion, 41–49. *See also* religious beliefs
Roof, Wade Clark, 53, 72, 80–81
Rosensaft, Menachem, 74–75
Rothberg, Michael, 108
Rubenstein, Richard, 73
Rwanda, 156–158

Sabbath, 55–56, 61, 89
same-sex relationships, 89
Scheff, Thomas, 42
Schindler's List, 101
Schwartz, Barry, 106–107
second-generation descendant identification, 27–29
seder meal, 59–60

selfhood, 31–32, 37–38
self-in-relation theory, 50–53
sexual exchange and survival, 34–39
Shekina, 75
Silbey, Susan, 14
Silverman, Kaja, 78
sites of terror/memorials and monuments, 105; acts of mourning at, 116–119; acts of remembrance and empathic bonding at, 120–124; identification with anxiety and fear at, 109–116; interactive dynamics of commemoration and sites of, 106–109; memory schemata for, 107; multidirectionality of, 108; universalism versus particularism and, 153–156
Six Days of Destruction, The: Meditations Toward Hope, 127
social memory, 108
Somers, Margaret, 14, 39
Sorrow and the Pity, The, 137
Soviet Union, 60–62
Spiegelman, Art, 140–144
spirituality, individuated, 72–78. *See also* religious beliefs
Stein, Arlene, 99
strength of spirit, 32–33
Sukkoth, 49
survivor panels, 130
survivors, Holocaust: descendants as research participants, 2–7; guilt, 46; heroism of, 33–34; international transmission of religious beliefs by, 66–68; moral identities and sexual exchange, 34–39; narratives (*see* narratives, family); as outsiders after the war, 99–104; rage toward God, 44–45, 66–67; seventieth anniversary of liberation of Auschwitz and, 9; victimized identities among grandchildren of, 24–29
Sznaider, Natan, 153

tattoos of grandparents' numbers, 91–92
Tibetan Book of Living and Dying, The, 77
trauma narratives, 19–29; about violence against women and girls, 22–23; heroism in, 29–34; inherited memories and, 23–24; told to children of survivors, 19–21; victimized identity and, 21–29
traumatic inheritance, 7–10, 23–24, 151; acts of mourning at sites of terror and, 116–119; anxiety and fear experienced at sites of terror and, 109–116; attachment and strain across generations, 83–86, 150; changing character of genocidal legacies and, 156–158; crisis of Jewish patriarchy and, 78–82; future directions in study of, 149–152; intergenerational tension, separation, and negotiating religious conflict, 87–92; ritual as site of posttraumatic emotion and, 41–49; self-in-relation theory of, 50–53; studies of, 13–14, 41, 83
Treblinka, 21, 119; descendants visits to, 112–113, 117–118; heroism in, 32–33
tropes of remembrance, 15–19
Turner, Victor, 42

Unitarianism, 57–58
universalism versus particularism, 153–156

victimized identity, 21–24, 149; among grandchildren of survivors, 24–29
Vietnam Veterans Memorial, 106–107
Vogel, Miriam, 116

Wagner-Pacifici, Robin, 106–107
Wardi, Dina, 25
Warsaw ghetto, 21
Weber, Max, 125
Wiesel, Elie, 127–128
women and girls: moral identities and sexual exchange by, 34–39; new ways of observing rituals among, 56; self-in-relation theory and, 50–53; violence against, 22–23, 157–158
Wuthnow, Robert, 53, 80

Yom Hashoah Vehagvurah, 126–127
Yom Kippur, 42–46, 54; anger toward God and, 44–45; loss of observance by survivors, 48–49; memorialization of lost family members during, 46–47; new approaches to observing, 54–55; survivor guilt and, 46
Young, James, 126

Zerubavel, Eviatar, 108
Zionism, 78

ABOUT THE AUTHOR

Janet Jacobs is Professor of Sociology and Women and Gender Studies at the University of Colorado. Her research focuses on ethnic and religious violence, gender, mass trauma, and collective memory. She is the author of numerous books and journal articles, including *Hidden Heritage: The Legacy of the Crypto-Jews* and *Memorializing the Holocaust: Gender, Genocide and Collective Memory*. Her most current work is on the intergenerational transmission of trauma in postgenocide societies and collective memory in Bosnia-Herzegovina.

www.ingramcontent.com/pod-product-compliance
Lightning Source LLC
Chambersburg PA
CBHW020413080526
44584CB00014B/1305